Also by Peg Tyre

The Trouble with Boys:
A Surprising Report Card on Our Sons,
Their Problems at School,
and What Parents and Educators Must Do

THE
GOOD SCHOOL

HENRY HOLT AND COMPANY   NEW YORK

THE
GOOD SCHOOL

How Smart Parents
Get Their Kids the Education
They Deserve

PEG TYRE

Henry Holt and Company, LLC
Publishers since 1866
175 Fifth Avenue
New York, New York 10010
www.henryholt.com

Henry Holt® and ® are registered trademarks of Henry Holt and Company, LLC.

Library of Congress Cataloging-in-Publication Data

Tyre, Peg.
    The good school : how smart parents get their kids the education they deserve / Peg Tyre.—1st ed.
        p. cm.
    Includes index.
    ISBN 978-0-8050-9353-7 (hardback)
  1. Education—Parent participation.   I. Title.
    LB1048.5.T97 2011
    371.19'2—dc22   2011009233

Henry Holt books are available for special promotions and premiums.
For details contact: Director, Special Markets.

First Edition 2011

Designed by Meryl Sussman Levavi

Printed in the United States of America

10 9 8 7 6 5 4 3 2 1

This book is dedicated to the men I love:
Peter, Mac, and Mose.

CONTENTS

THE
GOOD SCHOOL

INTRODUCTION

My parents used to say to me, "Tom, finish your dinner. People in China and India are starving."... I tell my daughters, "Finish your homework. People in China and India are starving for your jobs."

—THOMAS L. FRIEDMAN

WHY PARENTS NEED INFORMATION ON SCHOOLS. STAT!

There was a time when getting a decent education for your kids was pretty straightforward. You enrolled them in the local public school or you signed them up at the parochial or private academy their cousins attended. When you picked them up from school, you looked at the colorful finger paintings hanging in the hallways and noted what a warm and nurturing place it was. Once a year, you went to Parent Night in order to meet their teacher. Three times a year, you signed a report card. Somewhere along the line you might have made cupcakes for a bake sale, gone along on a class trip, or written a check for an annual fund-raiser. Your kids moved smoothly from elementary school to middle school to high school. Twelve years after you enrolled them in kindergarten, you sat on a folding metal chair beaming as they collected their high school diploma.

That era is gone. Long gone. These days, for better or worse, parents are required to do more—in fact, a whole lot more—in order to secure the best possible education for their child. And all over the country, parents are finding themselves in the uncomfortable position of knowing very little about education while making critical judgments about their children's schooling.

In many communities, parents, faced with an array of school choices, are growing frustrated and demoralized. After attending their fourth elementary-school Open House, Phoebe and Braken Hale reached the boiling point. Unfortunately, their story is all too common. Like most young parents, this Austin, Texas, couple care deeply about the quality of the education that their son, Rune, four, will get. But unlike most aspects of child rearing, where best practices are handed down from parents or discussed on message boards, over wine at the book club, or in countless books and magazine articles, they found that when it comes to schooling, good information is hard to find. The more Phoebe and Braken tried to learn about the school options for Rune, the less they felt they knew. Phoebe was partial to private schools, but the tuition was sky-high and the Web sites for the private schools in her area posted very little information about tests scores or their curriculum. Some new charter schools were generating a good buzz in the neighborhood but Phoebe, now an aesthetician, had taught in one and seen firsthand just how hard creating a successful learning culture can be.

Putting their trust in the process, Phoebe and Braken dutifully signed up and attended Open Houses for a charter school, a public school, a specialty public school, and a private school. All the schools looked decent. But on the school tours, the Hales and the other parents—even highly educated professional couples—seemed intimidated. No one, it seemed, wanted to ask hard questions: Why do the children get only ten minutes of recess? Why does the school favor one reading program over another? How do they handle kids who have behavioral issues? Phoebe was growing more anxious as the fall approached. She turned to a popular school-comparison Web site to see how her local public school stacked up. The standard-ized test scores seemed above average—about in line with the other schools in her area. The parent comments were neutral and guarded. Touring that school, she met the principal and received a list of skills upcoming kindergartners were expected to know before the first day. Resigned, the Hales opted to send Rune there. But as fall grew closer, Phoebe grew increasingly unsettled. She prides herself on making careful decisions about her family—and especially about the life of her child. "There just wasn't a lot of information about the academic program they were offering or what it would mean for my son," she said. "I lie awake at night wondering if I've done all I can do. After all, he only gets one chance at this."

There are other factors that have turned what may have once been routine decisions into high-stakes choices. Right now in this coun-try, parents with school-age kids are the best-educated group in his-tory. Many of us have personally benefited from increased levels of higher education, and even if we haven't, we understand the lasting value it confers. What is evident to almost everyone is that the manufacturing sector of the economy, once a font of solid, steady employment to workers lacking a college education, is rapidly van-ishing. There are fewer and fewer opportunities for those who don't do well in school. In the 1970s, according to a report compiled by the Center on Education and the Workforce at Georgetown University, nearly three-quarters of workers considered to be middle-class had not gone beyond high school. By 2010, that figure had dropped below 40 percent and has continued to shrink. Not only do highly educated people make more money than less educated ones, but the income gap between those who obtain a high school degree and those who get a college degree is growing larger every year. The Great Recession hammered that lesson home. Following the economic collapse of 2008, hundreds of thousands of people found themselves, abruptly, without a job. But not everyone suffered equally. In the second half of 2010, as the nation slowly emerged from the doldrums, the National Bureau of Labor Statistics found that the jobless rate for college graduates under the age of twenty-five was 8 percent. For high school graduates under age twenty-five who did not enroll in college, the jobless rate was a whopping 24.5 percent. These days, parents understand that finding or improving schools so that their children can be successful is the only sure ticket to anchoring them in the middle class.

Many of these same parents have also grown less trusting of educational professionals. In middle-class communities, that's partially a result of our increased levels of education. Back in our grandparents' day, the principal of our local school might well be one of the most educated individuals in the entire community, along with the town doctor, the local attorney, and the judge. The principal's word was sacrosanct. Today, parents who attend Curriculum Night in a suburban town may have as many advanced degrees hanging on the walls of their home office as the principal and superintendent who are addressing the crowd.

The growing fissure between parents and schools is also partially a result of the so-called accountability movement, which has tarnished our warm feelings about the superiority of the American education system. Since the Department of Education was founded in 1979, the federal government has been keeping close tabs on students' achievement levels. In the last twenty years, a unique combination of social justice types (concerned about the low achievement of poor kids) and fiscal conservatives (fretting about wasted tax dollars) have come together to force federal, state, and local governments, school districts, and schools into keeping closer tabs on how much kids are learning and how much it costs. In the last ten years, all that data—and comparative data from around the world—has coalesced into a sobering portrait. While some schools do a remarkable job and many more are adequate, a great number of kids—about a fifth in middle-class communities and up to half in poor ones—are not getting the knowledge and skills they need to succeed in life. And as Thomas L. Friedman has pointed out, our children will compete for jobs in a global economy.

According to the National Center for Education Statistics, spending for public schools has risen from $5,639 per child in 1980 to $10,041 in 2007 (these in inflation-adjusted dollars). Yet our reading scores have remained about the same: about a third of children in our public schools fail to become proficient readers. The World Economic Forum ranked the United States forty-eighth out of 133 developed and developing nations in quality of math and science instruction. The ACT administers subject tests to about 47 percent—some 1.57 million—of America's graduating seniors. From their scores, they determine whether or not students have enough base knowledge to get a B in a college-level course in that subject the following year. Last year's results were distressing: only three out of five high school graduates were prepared to tackle a college English course. Slightly less than one in four high school graduates—24 percent—were likely to pass colleges courses in the four tested areas: science, math, English, and reading comprehension. Private schools and parochial schools are not always the passport to success or the refuge from school failure that parents dream they will be. Not only do parents have to come up with the tuition, but all too frequently they have to counteract mediocre teaching by paying a phalanx of tutors to keep their children moving forward or risk having their child "counseled out." Even students from middle-class and affluent communities who appear to be doing just fine often exit the public school system with a diploma and big gaps in their education. Almost 30 percent of students who get accepted to a four-year university have to take remedial classes in order to do college-level work. Parents who might have once been content to cede power over their children to school authorities are getting a clear message: they need to take a much more proactive role to get their children the education they deserve.

Joe and Mary Ann Tarnoff, who live near Portland, Maine, didn't think they'd ever be the type of people to second-guess their daughter's teacher. Although they hate to admit it now, they used to view the "squeaky wheels" at their daughter's school with a combination of bewilderment and bemusement. In part, this is because they are a busy couple—he's a real estate agent and she's a lawyer—and have had neither the time nor sufficient knowledge to meddle with the way their local schools were run. When they enrolled their daughter, Francesca, at the neighborhood elementary school, they had no reason to worry. The test scores seemed good. But by the time she was in third grade, they began to wonder what was going on in Francesca's classroom. She was actively avoiding books and reading. Last November, they reviewed their concerns as they drove to the teacher conference. At the school, perched uncomfortably on scaled-down chairs, they listened to their daughter's fresh-faced teacher discuss the school's new reading program. When she finished, Joe asked, "So how does our daughter seem to like the new reading program?"

"All the teachers and students think it is fantastic," replied the teacher with great enthusiasm.

"How's our daughter's reading progressing?" Joe asked.

The teacher frowned, then, with seeming reluctance, opened her grade book.

"Well, it says here," she began, running her finger across the spreadsheet. Then she stopped. "Oh. That's interesting."

There was a long pause. Mary Ann and Joe leaned forward in their seats.

"We've had some concern about her reading ability," Joe explained. "She doesn't seem to like it very much. In fact, lately, she seems to avoid it."

"According to her recent tests, well, it doesn't seem like your daughter has made much progress from last year," said the teacher. Mary Ann's heart sank. In the spring of last year, Francesca's second-grade teacher told Mary Ann and Joe their daughter was barely on grade level.

"Well, I guess I'll have to have a discussion with our reading specialists about getting Francesca some support," the teacher said.

But, the teacher added, the reading specialist's schedule was so packed, it was unlikely Francesca would be able to get a formal evaluation before the first of the year. Coming up with an intervention program would, the teacher told them, realistically take months to put in place. Maybe by the spring? Then the teacher checked her watch. Another set of parents, eager to talk about their child's progress, knocked on the door for their scheduled parent-teacher meeting. By the time Mary Ann and Joe got to the parking lot, they had agreed that they were going to have to get a little smarter—and a lot more active—in their daughter's education.

The mounting pressure on parents to get and stay deeply involved in their children's education is not just a result of our higher standards: it is also a product of some well-calculated and long-term attempts to use parents' concern about their kids to force schools to change. Around the country, education reformers all across the political spectrum are hell-bent on transforming low-performing schools into something better. The central idea underpinning most of these reforms is that schools—and especially some public schools—are allowed to do a rotten job year after year because professional educators have a local monopoly on instructing our kids. Private and parochial schools can be a good option, but many of them are lackluster and often the ones that are good are beyond the financial reach of most families. If parents are given a wide variety of affordable, accessible schools to choose from, reformers believe, they will move heaven and earth to enroll their children in the best ones. Parents who are free to choose among different schools, the thinking goes, will unleash the powerful forces of the free market—and those forces will quickly wash away substandard institutions and better schools will grow up in their stead. No one knows if these theories will work, but the experiment is already under way and having a dramatic effect on education around the country.

Nowhere is that more evident than in the rough-and-tumble neighborhood of Compton, California, twenty-five miles and a world away from the glitz and glamour of Beverly Hills's chic Rodeo Drive.

There, parents like Marlene Romero have unexpectedly become foot soldiers in the battle for this new kind of school reform. Romero, thirty, a stay-at-home mom who recently went back to work, taking a job at Subway, sends her eight-year-old son, Ivan, to McKinley Elementary School, the public school a few blocks from her apartment. McKinley is, by nearly every measure, one of the worst public schools in the state of California. Without an opportunity to learn basic skills, the children who attend McKinley don't stand much of a chance: the district graduation rate is a shockingly low 46.8 percent, and only 3.3 percent of graduates were eligible to attend public universities in 2008. Romero was one of the district's casualties: she dropped out of school in tenth grade. Last fall, with help from some community activists, Romero and other parents of kids at McKinley decided to test a new school reform provision, the Parent Trigger, that had recently become law in California. They held meetings with other parents, explaining that the terrible test scores meant their children were not learning, and then they collected signatures on a petition demanding the school be turned over to the operators of a chain of high-performing charter schools. Last December, Romero and the others pulled the trigger. They boarded two specially rented busses and, in front of a battalion of national news reporters and television crews, presented petitions to the Compton Unified School District. Romero is no Norma Rae. Her days are filled with trying to do what it takes to keep the rent paid and food on the table. For her, pulling the Parent Trigger is a moral imperative. And her reasons for becoming active in her child's school resonate far beyond the confines of her troubled neighborhood. "As parents," she said in an interview, "it is our responsibility to get our children a good education. We want what is best for them."

The problem is that while we parents are being asked to play an increasingly pivotal role in our children's schooling, our knowledge about what makes schools effective is rudimentary at best. While McKinley's failings were easy to see, what most schools offer their students is more variable and the issues are more complicated. Parents of preschool through eighth-grade students are beset by difficult questions: How can I tell if a preschool is up to snuff? What should I be looking for when I'm on a school tour? What kind of math and reading instruction should my kids be getting? Does class size matter? And what about recess? It's got to be about more than just test scores, right? Or are test scores the bottom line? These are questions that often get hashed out around the local playground or at cocktail parties, but savvy parents understand that absorbing each other's impressions and alternately echoing each other's high-minded sentiments and abject fears do not, at the end of the day, help us make good decisions for our kids. We remain ignorant at our peril. The free market approach to school reform may or may not be successful, but it is creating plenty of tumult in a system of education long known for stasis. There will be winners and losers. And while plenty of smart people—from the Left and from the Right—believe the long-term impact on our schools will be a positive one, no one can deny that millions of kids will be on the wrong end of this dramatic transformation of American education.

Many parents—rich, middle-class, and poor—are struggling to find intelligent ways to engage, evaluate, and—when they can—improve schools, and their exasperation is palpable. "It seems like the principals are expecting us to choose a school for our sons while wearing a blindfold—pin the tail on donkey style," said Faith Vargas, a Detroit mother who, with her husband, has been looking at schools for their four-year-old twins. "It's absurd!" interjects Faith's husband, Bob. "When you purchase a house, you get an inspector's report. When you buy a sports car, at least you get to check under the hood. But now we are trying to do something that matters one thousand times more to our family than buying a house or purchasing a car—and what happens? We're expected to attend the Open

House, shake hands with the principal, blindly enroll them, and have faith that everything will turn out all right. We don't even get to look under the hood!"

If you are interested in "looking under the hood," this book is for you. It will help bring you up to speed on some of the most crucial issues and controversies that are likely to affect your child's education. It will provide you with a SparkNotes version of the history of education to explain to you why things are the way they are. It will introduce you to the freshest thinking—and some of the most innovative ideas—about how to help our kids do better. But more than that, it will help you judge the value of these ideas by providing you with the most solid research available. In areas where research is not yet clear, you will meet people and hear about research that will be creating headlines—and perhaps school policy—in the years to come.

The truth is, there is plenty of information out there. Razor-sharp people in Beltway think tanks and program directors at prominent foundations develop incisive analysis, publish position papers, and advise state and federal governments. But very little of it is written with parents in mind. Academics, too, have been scrutinizing the process of education for as long as we've had academics. There are people—and many of them are in the education business—who will reflexively dismiss all education research. They say things like, "There's research to support everything," as if no studies about education could begin to approach objectivity. And in some ways they are right: some education research seems more like advocacy. There are academics who fill journals with impressionistic studies that show that whatever pedagogical practice they favor—surprise!—works very well. For our purposes, that kind of research is of limited usefulness and will be considered only in passing. Happily, there are an increasing number of serious-minded and socially responsible academics who are keen to know what works in schools so they can replicate it, convince schools to adopt it, and encourage states to fund it. In the last twenty years, prestigious education organizations—some supported by the U.S. government and others by some of the wealthiest philanthropic organizations in the country—have begun subjecting educational practices to rigorous, objective studies. The results of the best studies could be very meaningful, if parents were aware of them.

But mostly, parents remain unaware. The strongest and most important studies are largely written for other academics and published in journals you are unlikely to find nestled in your pile of *New Yorker*s, *Real Simple*s, and *InStyle*s. Even if you found one or two that interested you—and I would invite you to call up a couple that are mentioned in the footnotes on Google Scholar—parents quickly encounter another roadblock: most studies are written in such thick jargon that reading a paragraph or two has about the same effect as a double dose of Ambien. There are also some powerful forces who are only too happy to keep you in the dark. Without going all *Da Vinci Code* on you, I would point out that textbook publishers have a vested interest in parents not looking too closely at what they are serving up to our kids. Some school administrators are less than eager to see parents get smarter. The fewer parents who know enough to rock the boat, the easier it will be to run a school.

I am not advocating one kind of school over another. There are deep divisions among people involved in education and I'm not a partisan for any particular side. For the last ten years, I've been writing and thinking about education, first as a writer for *Newsweek* covering social trends and education, then as the author of *The Trouble with Boys: A Surprising Report Card on Our Sons, Their Problems at*

School, and What Parents and Educators Must Do, then as a Spencer Fellow for Education Reporting at Columbia University, and lately I've been helping to teach young reporters how to cover education at the Graduate School of Journalism there.

In my capacity as journalist, I've had the opportunity to pore over a lot of education research. On a personal level, I've often reflected how valuable some of this material would have been to me at various junctures in my own life, when I was making decisions about my children's education. In a professional capacity, I've also spent a great deal of time in a wide variety of schools. I've seen ones that do a tremendous job educating class upon class of diverse students. But far too often, I've seen mediocre schools and sometimes really terrible ones. Heartbreakingly, I've sat with eager parents as they fill out endless application forms and seen hopeful parents line up for a high-stakes school lottery—the kind that many moviegoers saw in the documentary *Waiting for Superman*—hoping to get their children into the newest charter school or specialty program. Then, once the fanfare has grown faint, reality sets in. Well-meaning programs wither and fade. Although the charter school programs in *Waiting for Superman* get top marks, overall only 17 percent of charter schools deliver better results than the public schools that serve the same populations. They falter. And sometimes they close. Those children, once so full of hope and promise, quietly transfer to another program and parents struggle even more, trying to help them make up for instructional lost time. I've also seen parents exhaust their precious time and scarce family resources on a substandard private education for their children. I'm hoping this book will give you the tools to do better.

This book does not purport to be a blueprint for a perfect school. If I had a prescription for a system of education that I could guarantee would work for all our kids, you can bet I would be charging more—a lot more—for this book. And if you think about it for a minute, you'd agree that if someone tries to tell you there's a one-size-fits-all school formula that will ensure that two kids—the son of two biochemists from Darien, Connecticut, and the son of migrant farmworkers in Oakland, California—will both get into Harvard—well, that person is letting his enthusiasm eclipse our known reality. This book is not a comprehensive soup-to-nuts look at education, either. Instead, I've focused on seven essential domains of education that you need to know about now in order to help your preschool, elementary-school, and middle-school children. My hope is that these chapters will give you good tools to help you make decisions about where and how they will be educated. After reading this book, you may decide that you're still going to enroll your child in a school that is operating in a unique, unconventional, or untested way. Our family circumstances, our children, and our dreams for them are all unique. The goal of this book is to help you make the most informed decision possible. If you are going to take a risk, it will help you figure out just how big a risk you are taking.

One more cautionary note: some children—although probably not as many as we assume—have unique needs that are beyond the scope of this book. Very good resources exist for families of kids who have severe learning disabilities, autism, and physical and psychological disorders. This book is not one of them. If your child requires a specialized educational environment, though, you will still need to go through the process of finding the right school. Most of the topics in this book will be helpful to parents who are looking at schools that serve special ed, as well as mainstream, kids.

A word about the organization of this book: I've written about preschool first, which seems only natural. And while the other chapters are interrelated, the chapter on preschool can be read on its own. We all know that there are plenty of issues that come up in preschool—literacy, arithmetic, the balance of play and direct instruction, for instance, that will echo all through a child's education. We'll revisit some of those topics in more depth later in the book. But I'm betting if you have toddler, you don't have that much time to read. Even if you are a time management ninja and create a couple of empty hours to finish a book, I know that it is almost unfathomable to look at your adorable child, barely out of diapers, and focus your attention on the meaning of standardized test scores or the best approach to help third graders on their way to higher mathematics. If you are facing the first, and one of the most fraught, decisions—how to select a preschool—you can read the chapter on preschool and then put the book away for a year or so. I invite you to do just that.

For parents who have children entering kindergarten through middle school, the rest of the book is for you. I've organized the chapters roughly the same way most parents get informed about schools. Considering a school for your child? First, we hit the Web and check out the test scores. Chapter 2 is aimed at giving you a more sophisticated way to look at those numbers. Still interested in the school? We take a tour and eyeball the class size. Chapter 3 on class size will help you evaluate what you see. If we are really interested in the school, we speak to the principal or attend an Open House to try to learn what really happens inside the classroom. The chapters that follow, on reading, math, and scheduling, will give you an idea of what to look for regarding the curriculum and what kinds of questions to ask about the school day. Chapter 7 is about figuring out if the school you are considering for your child promotes quality instruction. It is very difficult for parents of prospective students to figure out if the teachers are good ones. Even parents of current students stumble here. This chapter will describe how to spot a good teacher and why getting your child a great teacher—and keeping pressure on schools to produce more—may be the single best thing you can do for your family and your community. Chapter 8 gives you a playbook for forming a constructive coalition with your child's school.

In some of these chapters, the evidence is in. In reading, for instance, there are certain practices that have been shown to be better than others. In other areas, open-ended and sometimes even contradictory strains of research need to be carefully weighed. This book will give you the opportunity to begin that process. In many of these chapters, I've delved a bit into educational history. Try to stay with me. I understand how precious your time is and how closely you must guard it. But the way schools are organized and the way teachers teach—how they explain things, what they emphasize, and what they omit—are done for some good and some not-so-good reasons. Some of our thinking about learning—traditions in pre-K education, for instance—can be based on ideas that are over a hundred years old. Other practices—replacing recess and break time with academic learning, for example—are relatively new. In order to support the best practices and discourage ones that are less effective, you should at least know where they come from. Each chapter will also include a section called "The Take Aways," in which the most important information is condensed to a few lines. I've also provided notes for every chapter. (The Notes section is at the back of this book.) You'll learn a lot from reading *The Good School*, but if you want to go even deeper into a particular subject, check out my Web site, www.thegoodschool.org.

Let me state unequivocally that I feel a deep admiration and respect for excellent teachers and brilliant principals. Being in the same room with an educational superstar feels like being on the bright side of the moon. The drive, energy, enthusiasm, and openness they bring to their work still dazzles me, even after all these years. Most of the best ones enjoy high levels of meaningful and intelligent contact with their students' parents.

Other administrators and teachers—the ones who occupy the many steps below excellent—sometimes seem like they are part of a conspiracy to keep parents in the dark. Nearly every administrator and teacher will tell you they are eager to have what they call "parent engagement"—especially around school trips and fund-raisers. But until recently, many people who run schools seemed unwilling to explain to parents why their teachers make the pedagogic choices they make—or even share basic statistics about the school, for example, the percentage of first graders who need extra support in reading or the number of teachers who leave the school each year—even though our children are the ones directly affected by those statistics and will succeed or suffer as a result.

In this book, you'll hear from many parents who have tangled with substandard teachers and administrators who seem bent on defending a system that is failing kids. I relate their stories to you in order to help you avoid the pitfalls that other families have stumbled into. But please keep this in mind: our schools and the teachers and administrators who work in them run the gamut from terrible to excellent. In these pages—and in our public discourse—we should not create comic book villains out of all the people who work in our education system. It is counterproductive. It is unrealistic. It is unfair.

In the chapter about teacher quality, schools of education are also, at times, cast in a harsh light. Frankly, some schools of education deserve it. The bad ones charge idealistic young people (mostly women) tuition and prepare them very poorly for the classroom. There are a great many people at all levels of government who would like to see the least effective schools of education revamped or closed. But that doesn't mean that all colleges of education are substandard. There are a number of schools of education that deliver thoughtful, relevant, and thorough teacher training. I hope the graduates from those excellent schools of education end up in your child's classroom.

Here's a good way to separate the good teachers and administrators from the not-so-good ones: the superstar policy makers, excellent school administrators, and highly effective teachers want you to have more information about education not less. They welcome parents who are prepared to enter an informed, constructive, and nuanced dialogue about what is happening to students. They are discovering that connected and satisfied parents—ones who are confident that schools are making good choices for their children—can become, in these difficult times, a school's staunchest allies. Principal James Bushman, head of the University High School in Fresno, a successful charter high school on the campus of California State University at Fresno, says finding informed parents is the key to his school's survival. For ten years, Bushman's staff has done a remarkable job educating five hundred ninth- through twelfth-grade kids and sending his graduates off to college. But getting parents to see what his school offers can be a challenge. "We don't have a lot of fat in our budget. We certainly don't have money for advertising," he says. As the operator of a charter school, he is barred from attending high school fairs given at local middle schools. UHS doesn't have a football stadium or sports teams that garner headlines in the local paper. A couple of times a year, Bushman organizes a comprehensive "information night" for parents of prospective students. His staff has a lot of information to share. "We are not a run-of-the-mill school. We are a super-duper hard-core college prep school. Our program is pretty specialized," he says. But in the early years, even getting parents in those chairs on information night was difficult.

Administrators and teachers at good schools want you to ask questions when you go on an Open House tour. They want you to have a sophisticated idea of what you should look for when you visit a classroom. They also have a lot of demands on their time. Out of respect for the job that teachers, principals, and superintendents do, it behooves parents to get smarter about schools. You can't reasonably expect them to educate you about education and do a great job teaching your child.

One of my heroes, education reformer Howard Fuller, the former Milwaukee school superintendent and now the director of the Institute for the Transformation of Learning at Marquette University, is a tireless campaigner for better schools, especially for low-income kids. He frequently writes and lectures parents about trusting schools and school authorities too much in what he calls the Happy School syndrome. "I've seen schools where there was lots of happiness. The teachers are happy. The kids are happy. The parents are happy. But you know what? In terms of academic achievement, the children are not doing well. And so I've asked them, 'Why are you so happy with your child's school when the children who attend here aren't doing well at all?' And the parents say they are pleased that the school is clean and safe and convenient. Now those things are important considerations. But you can't stop there."

Fuller continues: "Most parents know very little about how schools operate and what works. And if they had the time and inclination to sit down and read the latest research, they'd be stunned. It would be like finding out your doctor is taking out appendixes based on his own ideas of how appendixes should be removed. And even though the medical associations say, no, that is the wrong way to perform appendectomies, he still does it—and [is] risking the lives of his patients who come to him thinking he's using the safest techniques. There are some parents who do their homework. Who get informed. But there has to be a critical mass for things to change."

When it comes to school, we need to get savvier about the choices we make for our children. I'm hoping this book will be your first step on that journey.

CHAPTER ONE

THE PRESCHOOL SCRAMBLE

IN THE EARLY years of parenting, it seemed to Mai and Rush Ogden that the thorny questions never stopped coming. Of course, breast is best but is a sometimes bottle okay, too? Is Dr. Ferber a demigod sent to earth to preserve the sanity of new parents or a demon aiming to break the sacred bonds between parent and child? And what is the best way to lay down a time-out—one that hits the sweet spot between ineffectual finger wagging and Shock and Awe? When their son, Ian, turned three, the challenges of keeping him well fed, clean, dry, and safe gave way to long discussions about how to educate him. They weren't the only ones. The Ogdens realized that many of the thoughtful, well-educated couples they socialized with near their home in the Bay Area had become fixated on which preschool their child would attend. Neither Mai, a graphic designer, nor Rush, a mechanical engineer, who are both in their early forties, had attended preschool themselves. Mai set out to become an informed consumer. Already, Mai had found that parenting demanded that she balance short- and long-term concerns for her child. And choosing a preschool seemed to Mai to be a significant brushstroke in the Big Picture.

After talking to friends and a few weeks of virtual research, Mai had a short list of schools—four in all—that she wanted to visit. "There were several different kinds of schools but the one I was most drawn to marketed itself as a highly progressive program that stressed plenty of play. The Web site listed words like *developmentally friendly* and promised to teach kids what they were interested in," she recalled. After a series of school visits, Mai and Rush felt like they were pretty much back where they started. "I wanted to like the school that billed itself as progressive but to me it looked really disorganized. They made a huge deal about having a chicken for a class pet and growing food in their garden and then eating it— and that's all very nice—but the kids looked stressed out and the classrooms, which were filled with toys, were more like a messy playroom than a place for learning." To their surprise, the program they liked the best was a highly structured one that stressed academics. Children sat behind desks that were arranged in rows and faced the teacher's desk and a chalkboard. "It looked like an elementary school," says Mai.

Back home, the couple ran the tuition and fees for each program through their family budget; the prices were variable but one cost $15,000 a year and that was for a half day. They tried to figure out their best option. "It was a really hard, pressure-filled process," says Mai. "In the end, I realized that for all the research I'd done, and hours spent on school tours, I really didn't know what I was looking for or even the smartest questions to ask."

What kind of preschool should you choose for your child? It is a decision with big consequences. For many children, preschool will be their first opportunity to spend regular time with people who are not family. And, understandably, parents want to ensure that their child makes the transition easily. No one in their right mind believes that getting into a particular preschool (even the very best one in your town) will make a child a shoo-in for the Ivy League. Sorry to say, raising academically successful children isn't going to be that simple. And having a bad experience the first time out does not mean your child is doomed for school failure. Preschool, though, is the first footfall on a long and winding path toward becoming a well-educated adult. All parents want to do what they can to make sure that first step is a steady one.

If it feels like many of your friends are thinking, talking—okay, maybe even obsessing about this—it's because they are. A lot of middle-class kids now attend preschool. In 2009, according to the National Institute for Early Education Research, 47 percent of all four-year-olds, roughly 3.7 million kids, attended some sort of pre-school programming ranging from the federally funded Head Start, to state-supported preschools, to community-based for-profits, non-profits, and faith-based classes in church basements. Even as the Great Recession plays havoc with family budgets, the number of children attending preschool is growing. In moneyed urban areas— Manhattan, Los Angeles, Austin, Dallas, and the Gold Coast of Chicago—and in affluent suburbs, places where the population of advanced degree holders is most dense, getting into the right pre-school has become a competitive sport. And along with that level of anxiety come the predictable excesses. Remember the name Jack Grubman? In 2003, court documents revealed that Grubman, then one of the nation's leading telecom stock analysts, upped the rating of AT&T, a stock he was supposed to be monitoring, as a favor to Wall Street tycoon Sanford Weill after Weill donated $1 million to a prestigious Manhattan preschool to pave the way for Grubman's kids to gain admission. In the end, Grubman lost his job. No word whether his kids learned a lot at preschool that year.

Wealthy parents without those kinds of rich and powerful friends have turned to hiring preschool admissions consultants. Often retired preschool directors themselves or college admissions counselors making money in the "off-season," they charge anxious moms and dads between $500 and $12,000 to steer their toddler's acceptance into the right program.

Not all preschool anxiety is quite this cartoonish. But even well-grounded parents can get sucked into the madness that surrounds landing a spot in an affordable, high-quality preschool for their child. Michelle Howell, thirty-six, a marketing consultant, and her husband, Chris Miller, forty, who is in sales, applied to a number of preschools in their Austin, Texas, neighborhood when Michelle was pregnant with their daughter, Sydney. They thought they had the game beat when she was accepted to one when she was just an infant. But then, as Sydney grew, both her parents saw that she would benefit from interaction with other children before she was three years old—the age that their preschool of choice began. So they applied to a short list of twos programs. Their first-choice preschool program accepted Sydney to their wait list—and asked the wait list families to come to the school on a particular day at 7:00 a.m. Chris was traveling and Michelle's nanny starts at 7:30, but Michelle asked her to come early. "I figured I wouldn't be the first one to arrive," said Michelle. "But when I got there I found a couple of parents in chairs with blankets." One father showed up at midnight with a lawn chair, an extra sweater, and a cooler, as if he were waiting for tickets to go on sale for the Super Bowl. Three moms had gotten there at 2:00 a.m. Michelle and Chris were shut out. Their second-choice program also accepted Sydney to the wait list, but in the end the program's twenty-six spots for twos were filled by siblings of already-enrolled students.

Grandparents, watching their competent, usually rational sons and daughters grow bewildered and frustrated over preschool choices, are often confused. "I don't understand the stress," said Barbara Cohen, sixty-four, of Margate, New Jersey, who has watched her daughters, Dana, thirty-nine, and Stephanie, thirty-five, agonize over finding good preschools for Barbara's four grandchildren. "I think (my daughters) are getting caught up in a cycle: their friends are doing research and it's like a contagious condition. They stress more than necessary. They second-guess themselves. They question it. They rehash it." Back when she was a young mother, Barbara says, it seemed like there were fewer choices. She sent her children to the Jewish Y. "And that was it."

Barbara Cohen is right. There are more choices than ever before. What she may not realize is that for parents today, it pays to be particular.

BE CHOOSEY

When you visit a preschool, it's hard to see past the endearing and hopeful aspects of nearly any program. Four-year-old human beings—small, active, frank, wide-eyed, and endlessly curious—seem almost by design to fascinate and delight us. To the untrained eye, all but the most troubled programs look like reasonably happy places. What we know, though, is that all preschools are *not* created equal. There is good data to suggest that our gauzy and trusting perceptions of preschool can hide a troubling reality: there are badly run preschools or badly run classrooms within an otherwise acceptable preschool.

In his work at the Child Study Center in New Haven,

Connecticut, Walter Gilliam, a Yale University professor of child psychiatry and psychology, collects data from 3,898 preschools nationwide. In 2004, following a hunch, he added a few questions to the annual survey he sends to preschools, querying them about their expulsion rates. The results he collected shocked him—and later, the nation. It turns out that there are a whole lot of children who experience preschool—which should be a joyous phase of exploration and expanding horizons—as a dark time indeed. When he analyzed his data, he found that children in preschool are three times more likely to get expelled than children in kindergarten through twelfth grade. Expulsion rates were lowest in preschool classrooms in public schools and Head Start, and highest in faith-affiliated centers, for-profit child care, and other community-based child care settings.

Mark and Stacy Ambrose, thirty-five and thirty-two, respectively, who live outside of Nashville, Tennessee, didn't know kids could get expelled from preschool until it happened to their daughter. They were thrilled when their daughter, Marcella, entered the fours program run by an exclusive private school in their area. Stacy and Mark, who owns a chain of dry-cleaning businesses, weren't ready to commit to paying for private school from pre-K to year twelve. That decision depended on the economy, the profits from Mark's business, and if and when Stacy, a lawyer turned stay-at-home mom, went back to work. But they figured that enrolling their daughter in preschool at the school would give them a leg up in the competitive admissions process. Which made it all the more surprising when Marcella, who was initially thrilled at the idea of school, began to balk at going in the morning. "She's a spirited child and has strong ideas about how she wants to play, but she's a wonderful kid. We couldn't figure out what was wrong," says Stacy.

To get to the bottom of the problem, Stacy started staying late after drop-off, finding ways to "volunteer" in the classroom, and arriving for pickup time early. The teacher, she noticed, emphasized a great deal of quiet—sometimes even silent—seatwork. Each class had indoor and outdoor playtime, but Marcella's teacher spent nearly a half an hour marshaling the children for the two-minute walk to the outdoor play space. "I could hear the teacher barking commands all the time like 'line up,' 'walk in twos,' 'don't talk,' 'sit down,' 'don't fidget,' 'play quietly,'" says Stacy. "By the end of the day, Marcella seemed like a bottle of shaken-up soda, ready to fizzle over!"

While Stacy says she never observed the teacher yelling directly at Marcella, the teacher seemed frustrated with her child's unwillingness to follow her constant commands. Stacy worried that Marcella's behavior was becoming the focus of the class. Stacy asked for a meeting with the teacher, got nowhere, and then had a meeting with the preschool head, who told them that Marcella had trouble following directions, a trait the couple rarely encountered at home.

As weeks went on, the Ambroses' cheerful, happy daughter turned mopey and miserable. She argued with other children. One day, she even bit another child in class—something she hadn't done since she was a toddler in diapers. The preschool head called Stacy in and asked her to withdraw Marcella. "I couldn't believe my ears. She was getting kicked out! We were devastated," said Stacy. "It was horrible to think that she had failed at her first foray into formal learning."

At their best, preschools can improve kids' social skills and have some positive effect on children's academic achievement, at least in the early years of their education (the long-lasting effects are less clear). Many policy makers believe that preschool is a crucial part of a strategy to close the achievement gap between poor kids and middle-class kids by making sure that children from homes where reading and math are not emphasized get enough early learning to be ready for kindergarten. What often remains unacknowledged, however, is evidence that suggests that for some kids, preschool has a distinct downside. In a 2005 analysis, researchers at Stanford University and the University of California, Berkeley, found that kindergartners who had attended thirty or more hours of preschool every week were less motivated and more aggressive in class. Probably not the outcome parents were hoping for when they camped out overnight to make sure their child got a spot in a coveted program.

How do you determine which preschools to put on your short list? The first and most obvious step is checking out the Web site. But you may not get the best information there. For starters, some preschool programs can claim to be a certain kind of school and are actually certified as purveyors of that approach. Others can claim to be and aren't. For example, a preschool that calls itself a Waldorf school or a Rudolph Steiner program is evaluated by a governing body that measures that school against specific standards and practices. On the other hand, a school can call itself a Montessori program, and many do, without knowing a single thing about the educational philosophy developed by Dr. Maria Montessori.

The cursory "school tour" is often not that much more helpful. A smiling representative from the school describes a program as "developmentally appropriate," "play-based," "progressive," or "hands-on," and that seems reasonable enough when you are surrounded by other nodding parents. But when you are sitting alone in your car in the parking lot, you end up asking yourself, What does it really mean? How can we judge a program whose stated aim is to "improve school readiness"? It sounds good, but what the Ogdens at the start of this chapter discovered is that those terms can mean radically different things in different places. For example, preschools that claim to teach "reading readiness" run the gamut: a classroom where children are exposed to pictures of letters posted above the blackboard or a program where they are seated at a desk twice a day filling out phonics worksheets. Yet those different approaches to reading readiness could have a significant impact on your child.

In the pages that follow, you'll learn how to look beyond the boilerplate description to figure out what makes a quality preschool. First, we'll look at how ideas about early education have evolved. The preschool programs available to your son or daughter are a result of some deeply held—and in some ways deeply conflicting—views on childhood and childhood learning. It's helpful to know where some of these ideas come from before you can evaluate the three most important things about a preschool: the quality of the teacher, the quality of curriculum, and whether the school is delivering instruction in a way that is thoughtful, deliberate, and appropriate for your child.

By the end of this chapter, you'll have enough information to slice through the jargon on the Web site and look past the admissions director's sales pitch. You'll be able to fire off some meaningful questions during your school tour. You'll be able to analyze the underlying assumptions that the school is making about the kids they serve—and better figure out if it is a good fit for your family. By the time your child is ready to start preschool, you're still going to be filled with joy, hopefulness, anxiety, and a whale-size case of the oh-my-gosh-where-is-the-time-going nostalgia. But you'll also know a little bit more about what your child is getting into when she says good-bye and heads into her first classroom.

A SHORT HISTORY OF THE EDUCATION OF SHORT PEOPLE

Early education only became a large-scale enterprise in the beginning of the nineteenth century, and then, mostly for the poor. In those days, the custom was for young children from well-to-do families to remain in the care of nannies, nurses, and eventually tutors. But as more working-class adults in Europe sought jobs in factories, it became imperative to school poor kids—or at least keep them safe so their parents could earn a wage. Although we have few complete accounts of those first European nursery schools, many seem to have been grim affairs. The teachers didn't get any special training. The day was focused on what was called habit training and revolved around teaching the kids how to dress properly, do chores, say their prayers, and become literate enough to read a Psalter and sign their name. As anyone who has taken a course in European history knows, as cities grew, so did concerns about the degrading effects of the increase in population, poverty, disease, and pollution. Romanticism, which prized the natural over the mechanical and the intuitive over the logical, sprang up in response to those deep concerns created by a rapidly industrializing society. Romanticism, which held the free and untrammeled spirit of the child in great esteem, inspired not just some great poetry and paintings but also some interesting new thinking about nursery schools as well. Swiss educator Johann Heinrich Pestalozzi, and separately, in neighboring Germany, naturalist turned educator Friedrich Froebel, created schools that explicitly rejected the notion that poor children had to be "trained." Instead, the mission of their schools was to protect a child's spontaneous and creative spirit from the pressures of adult life. Classes should take place, the two educational philosophers believed, among trees and grass and birds. Students should handle tools and equipment made of natural materials. Pestalozzi allowed his students to play freely in the woods near his school with the expectation that his charges' innate curiosity would eventually fuel their appetite for formal learning. In Germany, Froebel, who became famous for coining the term *kindergarten*, wanted children to express what he called their activity drive—a thirst for exploration and learning—through play.

When European ideas about educating young children were imported to the United States by a handful of Lady Bountiful–type philanthropists, the tension between preschools that trained a child for adult life and preschools that purported to nourish a child's creativity and spirit came along with it. Those first American nursery schools were founded with a missionary zeal that owed more to the former than the latter. The kids who attended them were the three- and four-year-olds of poor and, it was tacitly understood at the time, morally inferior immigrant parents. The role of the school was to improve their habits in life so they could grow up and be better workers. Although some nursery schools taught basic reading and math, explicit academic instruction for young children was suspect. Scientific experts claimed that providing instruction to young children was downright dangerous and could lead to a kind of mental wasting. Back in 1838, Amariah Brigham, the director of the Hartford Insane Asylum, and an influential writer and speaker on social issues, warned that "mental excitement" brought on by early learning led to a disease called "precocity." Early learning, Brigham wrote, would "only serve to bring forth beautiful, but premature flowers, which are destined to wither away without producing fruit." Decades later, popular literature was still filled with Brigham's cautionary children—pale, bookish, and highly verbal youngsters who lacked the physical strength and stamina of their ruddy-cheeked playmates—and often succumbed to an early death.

In 1930, only .09 percent of sixteen million potential students—some very wealthy, most very poor—attended nursery school. In the 1950s, 84 percent of four-years-olds were still spending their days at home. Early childhood education was administered by mothers, family members, and neighbors, and, if families were rich enough, by nannies.

The post–World War II generation turned tradition on its ear. In 1965, the federal government started Head Start, which its founders promised would close what most policy makers were coming to realize was a yawning achievement gap between black and white children. Head Start became popular in poor communities, and soon middle-class women took note. Their massive shift into the workforce, which had begun as a trickle in the early 1970s, rapidly turned into a stampede. In the early 1970s, 60 percent of all mothers with school-age children stayed home—by the mid-1990s, 70 percent of women with school-age children were earning wages. In those early decades of the feminist movement, dads had not yet integrated child care into their job description. Harried, doing-it-all moms were fresh out of ideas about what to do with the kids when they were on the job. Preschools were a good option. In keeping with the times, most championed a "play-based" and "progressive" approach, which, ironically, often resembled the ideas espoused in turn-of-the-century Europe.

By 1990, preschool had become so common that in all kinds of communities it was considered the standard entry point into the American education system. What poor kids should be doing in preschool became the subject of a highly politicized debate. Conservatives, whose views were encapsulated in the 1994 book *The Bell Curve*, written by Richard Herrnstein and Charles Murray, had long argued that human intelligence is fixed at birth and invulnerable to change. Poor kids—especially black and Latino poor kids—lag behind middle-class kids in school, they argue, because they don't have the raw material to perform any better. Liberal educators countered that instead of less preschool, poor kids needed better-quality programs. They pointed to experiments like the High Scope program in Ypsilanti, Michigan, and the Carolina Abecedarian Project, which in the 1960s and 1970s provided high-quality preschool and, in the case of Abecedarian, wrap-around social interventions for poor kids and their families and then tracked the progress of the children as they grew into adults. Results from those studies began filtering out in the 1980s. In both projects, children who were randomly assigned to high-quality preschool did better in school (at least initially) and, later, made more money, got a better education, and were less likely to commit crimes than the kids from their community who didn't get the same intervention.

Around that time, new technology used in the burgeoning field of neuroscience was turning up some interesting data that dealt a near-fatal blow to the intelligence-is-innate faction and amplified the drumbeat for more academics in early learning, which reverberates to this day. Functional magnetic resonance imaging (fMRI) allowed scientists to "see" for the first time what was happening inside a child's working brain. And it was not what they expected. Many people had assumed that children were socially and physically active but intellectually dormant, waking up to learning as they aged. The fMRIs "showed" that our children's brains were on fire—burning glucose at a furious rate and laying down new neural pathways and pruning others. Stimulation enhanced brain activity in children—and, many believed, could enhance mental capacity. In April 1997, Hillary and Bill Clinton hosted the White House conference "Early Childhood Development and Learning: What New Research on the Brain Tells Us About Our Youngest Children" to convince elected representatives that early stimulation encouraged neurological growth and therefore that preschool programs that served poor kids should not be slashed. Journalists from television networks and major newspapers and newsweeklies broadened the message and it came out something like this: early academic learning is crucial in order to ensure that all children reach their full potential. The more the better.

Middle-class parents heard it loud and clear, and their interest set off an unprecedented marketing juggernaut. Whether it was a semester of pricey Gymboree classes, a Baby Einstein tape, a black-and-white "stim" mobile to hang over the crib, or a fill-in-the-blank workbook for three-year-olds—marketers told parents that these were essential tools children must have to meet their potential. By 2004, the market for so-called learning-and-exploration toys—which didn't even exist in 1980—rose to $510 million a year. The extraordinary growth has continued. In 2011, the worldwide market for "edutainment" toys—which now includes electronic "learning toys"—is expected to top $5 billion.

Any lingering doubts parents had about "precocity" went out the window. The more learning you could bring to your children early on, parents were told, the better off they'd be. Parents began to demand more academic-type learning in preschool. As the new decade dawned, many preschool classrooms began to look like scaled-down versions of fourth grade. Some divided the preschooler's day into academic subjects—just like high school. Others made "reading chapter books" their stated (if wildly aspirational) goal.

Some early childhood educators, particularly in affluent communities, vowed to resist the hype. Let the marketing geniuses play to parenting anxieties. Instead, they translated the old ideas of Froebel and Pestalozzi for a new hip generation, arguing that the toddlers who were allowed to play freely and explore the world today would develop into tomorrow's creative and intellectually curious students.

At the end of the twentieth century, the federal government released into this divided world a set of important reports based on new research on early learning. The findings of "Preventing Reading Difficulties in Young Children" and "The Reading Panel" were unequivocal: the central building blocks of literacy must be laid down before kindergarten. For the highly academic camp, this directive only added to their flash-card frenzy. The naturalistic play-based preschools took it as a matter of pride to ignore these findings. Reading instruction and even pre-literacy skills, the preschool operators cautioned, might be okay for children who come from disadvantaged backgrounds but middle-class parents risked their children becoming "hothouse kids" or "burning out" if they entered them in the academic rat race too soon.

Is it any wonder that young parents, most of whom want to send their children to preschool, are confused? They have good questions, for example: How much formal teaching and academics should preschoolers get? If they get too much, could they burn out? If they get too little, could they be left behind by their high-achieving peers? What does early learning really look like? It's hard to get good answers. Here's one place to start: when you are trying to find a good preschool, do what your mother always said—pay attention to the teacher.

THE GOOD TEACHER

The grown-up standing in the center of your child's very first classroom is going to be the key to your child's experience. Schools create the best possible environment for your child when they train their teachers well and hold on to the good ones for as long as possible. That's not always easy. It's an important job. But it's also a tiring job, and the pay is low. According to the U.S. Department of Labor, the median salary for preschool teachers is $23,070—but 10 percent of them made less than $16,030. It's not surprising that in many schools, the turnover is high.

You're not just looking for a school with decent teacher longevity, but also one with plenty of teachers to go around. According to the

National Institute for Early Education Research at Rutgers in New Jersey, preschool classes should have at least one adult per ten children, with an ideal class size of fifteen to eighteen kids.

When Mary Jane Webster, principal of the Barnum School, the preschool program for the public schools in Taunton, Massachusetts, sets out to hire a new teacher for her program, she has a long and detailed checklist. With the economy in the doldrums, Webster has an abundance of applicants.

The qualities she looks for? "A sense of humor, enthusiasm, and energy and focus," she says. "I'm looking for a preschool teacher who stands in the shower each morning and thinks about how she can connect with each and every child in her class and help them learn," says Webster.

How much do interactions between teacher and student matter? It turns out, a great deal.

Jen McIntyre, age forty, a stay-at-home mother of two, and her husband, Paul, age thirty-six, an attorney, sensed something was amiss shortly after they enrolled their daughters Eleanor and Ingrid in a nearby private preschool in Philadelphia. The school marketed the fact that it did not buy into the "rat race" mentality of early schooling, with all the "test, test, test." "I felt like the school would let my kids have an academic experience but also protect their childhood," says Jen. From what she could tell, the preschool provided the kind of warm and nurturing environment that Jen had enjoyed when she herself had attended preschool. She also liked that the children were in mixed-age groups. But after a few weeks, Jen began to wonder if the school was in some sort of tumult. Jen reflects on what she saw. "The teachers in both my girls' classrooms seemed like they were strained—and remote from the children. Eleanor's teacher seemed particularly disconnected from Eleanor," says Jen. "I was so concerned that I mentioned it to other parents, who confessed that they had the same concerns." The mixed-age group, which had appealed to Jen, turned out to be large—about thirty kids and two teachers. The dynamics of the group devolved as the year went on. "The teacher didn't seem to care what was age-appropriate for the children. She took a kind of 'let's see what happens' approach." What happened was this: one of the older kids began to behave aggressively toward her daughter Eleanor. Jen started to fret.

"I was so worried about Eleanor psychologically—I felt like she was bullied by older kids and neglected in the classroom." It was worse for Eleanor's younger sister, Ingrid. Her teacher was cold and harsh. "Ingrid responded by being very defiant," which only seemed to make the relationship between her little daughter and her teacher worse.

Study after study shows that early child-teacher relationships are key. In 2001, researchers found that children who had good relationships with their preschool teachers entered kindergarten with happy, positive feelings about school. Those positive feelings made it possible for them to make new friends more easily, gain peer acceptance, and form a warm bond with their kindergarten teacher. These favorable relationships in turn predicted high achievement throughout elementary school. The same study reveals that the inverse is also true. Negative relationships between a child and teacher in preschool can cast a pall over the teacher-child relationships in kindergarten and set the stage for academic and behavioral problems through eighth grade. Poor early teacher-student relationships can turn even gifted kids off to school: researchers found that poor-quality teacher-child relationships in the early years hurt kids' achievement even when the study controlled for IQ.

What should you look for when you meet your child's potential preschool teacher? The American Psychological Association has some specific suggestions: a teacher should show pleasure and enjoyment of her students; interact with them in a responsive and respectful manner; offer students assistance in a timely way; help them reflect on their thinking and learning; demonstrate knowledge about students' backgrounds, interests, and emotional and academic strengths; and seldom express aggravation and irritation with students. In short, your child's first teacher is going to have to be one of those highly tolerant and relentlessly positive people who can be kind to your child on the days when it is sunny and your child is laughing and ready to learn, and on stormy days, too, when your young scholar is upset, overtired, and cranky.

And as for Jen McIntyre? To her relief, her children are bouncing back. She decided to change preschools, and when she attended the next round of Open Houses, she made sure to observe teachers in the classroom. She says, "I was so naive. I really had no experience in choosing a school. I didn't really know what I should look for. I was looking at schools more superficially than I ever would now."

The teacher or teachers in a good preschool classroom also need to talk a great deal and to talk very clearly. One of the very best things a preschool experience can give your child is an opportunity to speak, hear, and sing words.

Why the emphasis on spoken language? The more children are spoken to, the more they themselves speak. And the more they speak, the greater their vocabularies. The greater their vocabularies, the better their reading fluency and reading comprehension is likely to be. We'll talk about reading in more depth in chapter 4, but the central concept is that in general, the more words your child speaks, hears, and comprehends, the more readily she will understand those words when she encounters them in print.

We have two behavioral scientists, Betty Hart and Todd Risley, to thank for a big chunk of our understanding of just how important the spoken word is to the cognitive development of children.

In fact, parents have a lot to thank Hart and Risley for. In the 1960s, Hart, Risley, and another famous child behavior expert of his day, Montrose Wolf, worked with the University of Kansas to set up a preschool intervention program in a high-poverty neighborhood in Kansas City. The three of them cooked up a practice of allowing kids space to cool down—what has become known to every parent as the time-out. But they did more than change the way parents dealt with their ornery children. In the early 1990s, the two researchers were connected to a preschool that served kids from poor and working-class families in Kansas City. The kids in their program, like most poor and working-class kids, used fewer words, had smaller vocabularies, and did less well in school than children from middle-class communities. So Hart and Risley set out to build the children's vocabularies. They asked teachers both from the poor preschool and from a preschool nearby that was attended by professors' kids to take students on field trips—to a bank, for instance—and then had the teachers hold discussions about banking, tellers, deposit slips, and cash cards. A trip to the zoo was followed by a discussion of fur and scales, animal families and habitats. Then Hart and Risley measured the poorer kids' vocabulary growth and compared it to the vocabulary growth for middle-class students. The experiences seemed to be expanding for both groups. But they found that the wealthier a child, the greater his rate of word acquisition. Hart and Risley saw that while preschool teachers could teach underprivileged kids more words, they could not seem to accelerate their rate of acquisition. This meant that no matter how many trips the teachers took these kids on—to banks, to zoos, to country fairs, and to the park—the poor kids could never catch up.

Hart and Risley wanted to know more. What is the turning point that sets certain four-year-olds on a path to become pint-sized connoisseurs of language and keeps others tethered to a small, restrictive vocabulary? And when exactly does it happen? To find the answers, Hart and Risley selected forty-two families of newborns from across the economic spectrum. They spent the next two and a half years observing what was said to them in their homes. Starting when the children were seven to nine months old, the researchers observed, recorded, transcribed, coded, charted, and analyzed nearly every utterance between the parents and child until the child turned three. In all, they recorded more than thirteen hundred hours of casual interaction between parents and their children. The familial tableaux in wealthy households and the poor ones were parallel: parents from all walks of life nurtured their children, played with them, talked to them, disciplined them, taught them manners, instructed them on how to dress and how to use the toilet.

But there were important differences. What they found was partially what they expected to find: the wealthier and more educated families spoke more to their children. The results that staggered Hart and Risley, and later the world of educational researchers, was the differential between the professional work and poor families. Using the data they collected in those homes, Hart and Risley projected that in the first four years of life, children in a professional family would have heard or spoken 45 million words. Working class kids would have heard 26 million words. Welfare families? A mere 13 million.

But there's more: all parents used similar imperatives and prohibitions—as you might expect, parents from every walk of life say, "Come here," and "Stop that," and "Don't put your fingers in your nose," to their kids. But the wealthier the parents were, the more extraneous talking the parents did with their kids—asking open-ended question like "What do you think will happen?" or "What are you doing?" and discussing feelings, presenting activities, and describing past events. The combination of lots of words and a general willingness on the part of these parents to use language in a descriptive, consoling, productive, and connecting way, pushed down the gas pedal on their kids' rate of word acquisition. It is a priceless gift. Six years later, Hart and Risley looked at twenty-nine of the forty-two children again to see if the rate of vocabulary growth would predict performance in school. It did. The three-year-old test subjects who had the highest rates of vocabulary growth turned into third graders with the strongest language skills and highest reading comprehension.

Good preschools know that critical skills are developed through speaking, listening, and open-ended conversation in the home, and are eager to provide more of it during the school day. Well-run preschools that serve underprivileged kids know they could be fighting against a deficit. But those who enroll students from middle-class families know, too, that technology may be turning Hart and Risley's research on its head. Children in affluent families now "play" on screens instead of talking with parents, caregivers, or others. Leapster is the so-called educational toy de jour. Parents who once narrated the view as they pushed their children in a stroller now push the stroller silently with telltale white wires hanging from their ears. Instead of listening to a parent describe the attributes of a neighbor's dog and cawing "dawg!" or "woof," or exclaiming "soft fur!" toddlers are likely to be occupied flicking through apps on Mom's iPhone. Quality time between parents and toddlers is often punctuated by Mom and Dad whipping out their BlackBerry and sending a text or four or five, a habit that further reduces opportunities for children to overhear and engage in conversations. Middle-class kids may not be acquiring the same number of words that Hart and Risley once predicted. And their reading comprehension rates may in time reflect it. Good preschools need to put a huge emphasis on learning new words by hiring teachers who have good vocabularies, love to tell stories, and are excited to introduce children to an array of new words (and ideas!) every day.

THE TAKE AWAYS

1. Look for teachers who are responsive to and respectful of their little students. Teachers should seem to know each child well—and be familiar with their strengths and background.

2. Beware the crabby preschool teacher. Preschool is no place for sarcasm, sharp tones, or any version of tough love. Yes, supervising a gaggle of four-year-olds could bring a strong man to his knees. But preschool teachers should take obvious pleasure in their young scholars.

3. Look for preschool teachers who talk, talk, talk, and create opportunities for students to do the same.

ELLO-MENO-PEE, 1, 2, 3, OR HOW PRESCHOOLS CAN HELP YOU (REALLY) TEACH YOUR BABY TO READ

There are skills in pre-literacy and early math that children need to be developing and refining in the preschool years to ensure they'll do well in school later on. Don't panic. They aren't complicated. But they are crucial. Many preschools are well aware of them. But some are not.

Everyone knows we need to read to our children early and often. And your child's preschool teacher should be doing the same. How much is too much? There doesn't seem to be an upward limit—although children have limited attention spans. When it comes to reading to children, the bulk of the research concludes: the more the better. Reading to preschool children increases that all-important rate of word acquisition by surrounding them with English language sounds. It helps even more if your child's preschool teacher points out words as she reads so kids get the idea that those black marks on the page actually stand for the words that the teacher is saying and ideas they are hearing. It can be puzzling—to literate teachers and parents the concept of the printed word seems obvious. But for some kids, even kids with teachers and parents who read to them a lot, the idea that symbols represent ideas comes slowly.

Your child's preschool teacher should also be making a very big deal about the alphabet song and those twenty-six characters. In several classic studies, fluent letter-naming is shown to be a good predictor of reading achievement, not just in kindergarten or first grade, but right through the seventh grade. There are several reasons for this, but among the most important, recognizing letters makes it easier to figure out letter sounds—which you'll see in chapter 4 turns out to be one of the giant steps in the sometimes-laborious process of learning to read. Preschool teachers should also be helping kids identify colors, reciting numbers in sequence, teaching them to understand the concept of numbers, even naming animals. Your child's ability to look at a picture of a cow and quickly and accurately come up with the name of that farmyard bovine helps teachers make sure some complicated brain functions they'll need for reading are already online.

Researchers tell us that one of the fundamental differences between kids who learn to read well and kids who don't is this: the former can discern individual words in sentences and sounds within those words. Kids who are likely to struggle have a hard time hearing different words in a sentence and struggle to hear the *cah* as an individual and distinct sound in the word *cat*. It has nothing to do with intelligence. The ability to discern sound seems to reflect some basic differences in neurological wiring. But those skills can and should be strengthened throughout your child's preschool experience.

It sounds complicated, but in practice it's not *exactly* brain surgery. First off, children need to hear that sentences can be broken into sound chunks—words—and later, even smaller sound chunks, what in many cases turn out to be syllables. Singing lyrics and tapping out the beats for words turns out to be a painless way to build those skills.

Not all at once, but definitely by the final year of preschool, children should understand that sound chunks of words can be switched around at will. Most children get infectious pleasure from the sound manipulation that goes into the nonsense rhyme "Hickory, dickory, dock. A mouse ran up the clock." In linguistic terms, they are, in fact, doing something sophisticated and crucial—splitting the first sound from the rest of the word and substituting another sound.

Do you really have to pay attention to what, at the end of the day, boils down to your child's ability to sing nursery rhymes? Yeah, I'm afraid you do. The ability to hear and manipulate sounds, which reading experts call phonological awareness, is essential for school success, and for many kids it is a learned skill. In one test conducted in the late 1980s over the course of a preschool year, children in the treatment group engaged in a variety of games and activities: nursery rhymes, rhymed stories, investigation of word length, clapping and dancing to syllabic rhythms, solving puzzles posed by an imaginary troll who spoke only in a syllable-by-syllable manner. Kids in the control group had a regular preschool experience. At the end of the year, they could all identify the initial word sound (that *buh* is the beginning sound of the word *bat*) and final word sound (that *tuh* is the last sound of the word *bat*). The treatment group could rhyme better— they'd had a lot of practice—but neither the control group nor the treatment group showed a clear advantage in learning to read. In grade one, the kids who got "treated" with rhyme games and the syllable-talking troll tested better in word recognition and spelling. By second grade, the treated kids dominated the control group in word recognition and spelling. Three years after the troll had spoken his last, the treatment group read better than the control group and their rate of improvement was not waning but picking up speed.

Too often, reading experts say, children do not get this simple kind of training in preschool. They enter kindergarten behind other kids who have been taught it or picked it up spontaneously. Absent an opportunity to practice it, kids who don't have it are retained in kindergarten—too often with another teacher who doesn't offer enough practice, either. In study after study, most kids given an opportunity to build a weak phonological sensitivity into a strong one can do it. But if they don't get that chance, they often struggle profoundly throughout their school years.

There is less consensus among researchers about how to prepare children to be successful in math. But what is becoming clear is that we ignore our children's early math education at their peril. In chapter 5 I'm going to delve into some of the most innovative thinking about how we develop a numbers sense and why certain kids seem to warm to math more than others. When your child is preschool age, what you need to know is this: there is no need to wait until children are older and are able to think and speak in more abstract ways to introduce math concepts. A certain kind of math ability seems to be innate in all of us and has been measured days after birth. Although we all have different levels of inborn math sense, a child's agility in math depends on prior experience. And one experience in math builds on another. In the years before preschool, you should be spending a lot of time counting fingers and toes, Cheerios, streetlights, teddy bears, and blocks. Preschools and parents need to work together to reinforce concepts like greater than and less than and bigger and smaller. Preschools should be reinforcing the number concept (as in "How much is three?") and introducing measurement. There is growing evidence to suggest that early math exposure is key to helping our children succeed in mathematics all through school. Don't like math? Shhh. As you'll read in chapter 5, your negative or fearful attitude toward math could hurt your child's chances of success.

THE TAKE AWAYS

1. During a typical preschool day, teachers should be reading to children. And not just once in a while.

2. Numbers. Letters. Colors. Farm animals. Your child should be naming them all. Repeatedly.

3. Paging Dr. Seuss! Rhyming is critical. Song lyrics, poetry, and rhyming games are good, too.

4. Math knowledge builds on math knowledge. Time to start talking about bigger than and smaller than, first, second, third, and last. Number games, sorting, and measurement.

FINDING THE RIGHT BALANCE

In preschool, delivering the right combination of learning and free play is critical. In some quarters, play is the thing. Parents who even ask whether preschools are preparing students for reading and providing lessons in early math are treated as overaggressive. "We don't push children here," one preschool head told me recently when I inquired whether her teacher knew the kinds of skills children needed to develop in order to read. "We don't believe in it." And at the other pole, highly academic preschools are not hard to find, either: chairs and desks are set up in rows, children are given worksheets, and there is hardly any space in the room or time in the day for exploration. Avoid the extremes. Strictly academic-type preschool environments consistently produce kindergartners and first graders who know more. But their academic advantage fades by third grade. And there are suggestions that teaching preschoolers as if they are third graders can create problems for them later on. In a study conducted in the late 1960s as part of the HighScope Perry Preschool Project in Ypsilanti, Michigan, sixty-eight poor children were randomly assigned to three different kinds of programs: one where teachers focused on getting kids to provide correct answers to academic questions, another a play-based nursery school, and a third whose program mixed skill and play. Researchers showed that the academic approach initially prepared children better for kindergarten, but over time, the children who attended highly academic preschools reported more emotional problems, admitted more acts of "teen misconduct," and had lower academic aspirations than the kids who attended the playful learning program. They even found that kids who received direct instruction in preschool were much more likely to be arrested, although to the average observer the connection between stealing a car or assaulting your neighbor and the kind of preschool class you attended seems pretty thin. Another, smaller study on a different group of youngsters also suggested that highly academic preschools, while initially raising the academic achievement of all children, can depress it over time, and reduce the long-term achievement for certain kinds of kids, particularly boys.

The very best preschools display a more subtle kind of instruction, with teachers who work on three levels: they know what kids need to learn, they know how to break it down into manageable chunks, and they build these skills through fun activities that strengthen pre-math and pre-literacy-type learning.

Mary Jane Webster, that Massachusetts preschool principal whom we met when she was reviewing résumés, says the best

47

preschool teachers turn out to be ones who are very smart. "There's a lot of things that you have to figure out. Preschool can be more difficult than the other grades because a lot of your teaching has to be embedded in other things. Understand that when you're playing with one child you're working on their vocabulary, and with another child that you're facilitating social skills and you're teaching it through indirect ways."

Margee Ready, director of St. Paul's preschool in Fairfield, Connecticut, says that once parents are shown the difference between academic-type learning and learning embedded in play, they often embrace it. Not long ago, a husband and wife made an appointment with her to discuss their worries that their son was lagging behind in his pre-reading skills. "They were deeply concerned that their son hates doing his flash cards," says Ready with a laugh. "So I told them, 'Don't do the flash cards!'"

Teachers at Ready's school use a game to help teach alphabet awareness. Her teachers make two sets of laminated cards, each one with a letter of the alphabet on it. Half the cards are spread on the floor. The other half are put in a deck and children select them randomly, then run down the length of the room and match it with one of the cards on the floor—shouting out the letter name the whole time.

"We know this kind of learning is better than flash cards," she says.

Skills-based play activities such as this need to be balanced with free play. In many preschools free play—where children are able to run, jump, build, play games, and put on costumes and pretend—is an increasingly rare commodity. In a study of three low-income, community-based child care centers, researchers found that in 1982 social pretend play for 4.5-year-olds accounted for about 41 percent of the school day. In 2002, social pretend play had dropped to 9 percent.

The epidemic of highly structured preschools, which edge out free time and imaginative play, has grown so widespread and so worrisome that doctors have begun to sound the alarm. In 2006, the American Academy of Pediatrics issued a position paper stressing the role of play in healthy child development, and specifically suggesting that families choose child care and early education programs that meet children's social and emotional developmental needs as well as prepare them to achieve academically.

Temple University psychology professor Kathy Hirsh-Pasek has watched the transition toward more academic preschools with growing unease. As the director of the Infant Language Laboratory and an author of eleven books on child development, she knows better than almost anyone else how kids learn. And she's worried about the way play is being neglected in preschool education. "In an effort to give children a head start on academic skills such as reading and mathematics, play is discouraged and didactic learning is being stressed," she says. "Play has become a four-letter word."

PLAYING TO SUCCESS

There's a playful preschool program called Tools of the Mind that is creating a big stir in early education circles. Its aim is to use play to help kids learn academic skills—the ones that lead to proficient reading and math. But even more critically, the program uses playful activities to help strengthen focus, self-regulation, and working memory—skills that social scientists now say may determine whether smart kids are successful in school or not. I've included it here because finding out about the ideas that are the foundation of Tools of the Mind expanded my view of what I thought of as an excellent preschool.

The fascination with the program comes, at least in part, from a growing recognition that narrowly focused, academically driven education puts limits on young children. "After years of pouring millions of dollars and thousands of hours into getting our children to learn content—numbers and letters," says Tools of the Mind cofounder Deborah Leong, a professor at the Metropolitan State College of Denver, "we, as a society, are coming to a conclusion that it is not working. The kids who get the most intensive intervention are not showing long-term gains."

Intellectual ability without self-regulation, it turns out, is like a Porsche with a lawn mower motor. Flashy? You bet. But it's not going to take you very far. What we used to consider soft skills, like the ability to focus, to drown out distractions, to plan, and to persevere, are starting to seem like bedrock traits for sustained and lasting achievement. And research bears this out: kindergartners, for example, who show high levels of self-regulation do better in school than kids who know a lot of letter and numbers or who have a high IQ.

We've known this for a while. In the now famous marshmallow experiment, Columbia University professor Walter Mischel showed the impact of one of those so-called executive function skills on school performance. Back in the late 1960s, while a professor at Stanford University, Mischel tested 653 four- and-five-year-olds— many of them children of Stanford professors who attended nursery school in nearby Palo Alto. He was trying to determine their baseline levels of self-control. A researcher brought each child into a room, let them play with some toys, and then seated them at a desk with two marshmallows and a bell. The researcher gave the child an option. The researcher explained that he was planning to leave the room. The child could (a) wait until he returned, at which time she could eat two marshmallows, or else (b) ring the bell and the scientist would reenter the room, but the bell ringer would only be allowed to eat one marshmallow, not two.

Kids reacted in different ways. Some could not wait more than a few minutes. Others could wait fifteen minutes or longer. Of the kids who could wait, many used strategies like covering their eyes or distracting themselves so they didn't think about eating the marshmallow. When Mischel and his team followed up on the kids—at fifteen and again at eighteen—they found that the kids who could wait did better on their SATs—210 points better—than the fast bell ringers. And their parents described them as less stressed, less rattled by frustration, and more able to plan for the future.

Scientists (and most parents) have observed that children seem to have different levels of self-regulation. In the last decade, some researchers have become convinced that self-regulation is like a muscle that can be strengthened.

The Tools of the Mind program provides opportunities to strengthen those skills. How does it work? In the last two years, the littlest learners in an old but well-maintained public school in Hoboken, New Jersey, across the Hudson River from Manhattan, have been on the cutting edge of preschool education. Under the watchful eyes of experienced trainers, and five teams of federal researchers studying the program, the teachers have been running kids through a series of Tools of the Mind activities aimed at teaching early literacy and numbers skills but, most critically, improving their self-control, extending their ability to hold directions in their mind (what psychologists call the working memory), and helping them harness their ability to focus.

On a bright autumn morning not long ago, the preschool classroom looked pretty much like any other standard classroom. There was no fancy technology or, in fact, any electronics at all save for a dusty television hanging, forgotten, from the wall. No stack of spanking new textbooks. Nothing to indicate that a revolutionary new kind of instruction was under way. Instead, sun poured in the wide windows onto four small tables with small chairs pushed around them. There was a multicolored rug surrounded by shelves loaded with books, blocks, and art supplies. One entire corner was given over to dramatic play.

Teachers build the children's self-regulatory skills by subtly shifting the way they move the children through familiar, everyday preschool-type tasks. For example, it is morning meeting time and the eighteen children and two teachers are naming the day and charting the weather just like kids in preschools all over the country. Unlike other preschools, where individual children might be encouraged to raise a hand and provide an answer to the teacher while others listen, the eighteen children in Tools of the Mind classes answer the question "What is the weather like today?" in a chorus of voices, all at the same time. There is a reason for this. "We don't believe children actually listen to each other very well. That's a skill that we need to help them build," says Amy Hornbeck, a former teacher turned Tools of the Mind researcher who now coordinates some of the Tools of the Mind programs for the state. "Early in the year, when one is answering, the others just space out. We don't want to give them that chance." Answering all at the same time forces them to keep their attention focused longer than they might—and at four years old, adding a few seconds on to a child's attention span can feel like a Herculean task.

Although it is autumn, and the students are still regarding one another with a degree of wariness, circle time is followed by what has already become a classroom favorite: freeze dancing. Eighteen four-year-olds dance to rock and roll while the teacher holds up a twenty-four-inch laminated card with a stick figure. This one has its stick arms turned up at a ninety-degree angle. After about sixty seconds of frenetic movement, the second teacher switches off the music and the children are supposed to raise up their arms to mirror the laminated stick drawing. Some of the children, especially the ones who were in Tools of the Mind classrooms as three-year-olds, mimic the drawing exactly. Others seem unable to keep the arms-raised image in their minds, or if they can think of it, they might be struggling to adjust their bodies accordingly. The teachers help those kids by manually pushing their arms into the right position and then the music starts again. Hornbeck nods. "This is to help children regulate their bodies."

In another preschool classroom, children have culminated a period of storytelling about freckles by dotting a white dry eraser board with thick markers. When the teacher turns on the music, they say the word *freckles* and draw freckles. When the teacher turns it off, they cap their markers and raise them over their heads. Some kids can't make more than a dot or two before they begin scribbling aimlessly. The teacher reminds the students who are scribbling to go back to dot making, and, in a key bit of scaffolding, reminds them to murmur the word *freckles* as the marker hits the whiteboard. (In the Tools of the Mind program, teachers instruct children to use self-talk to stay focused and on task.) A few feet away, another student neutrally redirects one of the scribblers to "make freckles."

Later on, the same group of children will plan their play—drawing pictures of themselves. In one case, two boys decide to be road repairmen. After declaring their intention to inhabit that role, they go to dramatic play and begin to build roads with blocks. A few minutes into the game, the boys put all four hands on the same block and begin to tug. For a moment, it looks like a confrontation will break out. But the most aggressive-seeming boy quickly reverts to his fantasy role as road repair foreman. "Let's lay down that road there," he says. And the other boy, reminded that he is part of the crew, begins road construction again.

Planned, extended dramatic play—what Leong calls "mature play"—is where children learn the most. "In most preschools you see children sampling activities, literally flipping from one thing to another. The opposite of this—mature play—is very different. Mature play is what most parents engaged in when they were young kids. They dressed up and played mommy, daddy, soldier, cowboy . . . whatever. They played for hours and hours and days and days." In Tools classes, children adopt play scenarios with multiple roles and clearly defined rules, which they make up on their own and describe out loud to each other. (You're the shopper. I own the grocery store.) "If you ask six-year-old children to inhibit their movement, many will struggle to do it," says Leong. "But the same child, engaged in a fantasy scenario, can stop themselves from doing things that are not part of the role." Fantasy play, set up the right way, allows them to effortlessly flex their self-control. That strengthened self-control can then be brought to bear in other domains of life, including academics.

Tools of the Mind has been a revelation to Elizabeth Schwartz, a teacher with thirty-five years of experience. Starting was difficult. The training was thirty hours long. "There is a lot of preparation and a lot of rethinking that teachers need to do because Tools is not a new curriculum, it is a new way of thinking about learning," says Schwartz. The troubleshooters that Leong and her nonprofit group sent to help the teachers adapt Tools to their Hoboken classrooms helped. By the middle of the first year, Schwartz was a believer. In her classroom, the Tools of the Mind program reduced behavior problems, helped the children improve their focus, and transformed even rambunctious kids into capable, self-possessed students.

Researchers who are combing through every aspect of Tools of the Mind are coming up with impressive numbers that back up Schwartz's assessment. According to a paper published in 2007 in *Science*, the Tools of the Mind program has been effective in strengthening the executive functioning—skills that educational researchers recognize as fundamental to school success.

THE TAKE AWAYS

1. Preschoolers don't learn like third graders. All learning must be embedded in play.

2. Worksheets? Students sitting at desks or on the floor at circle time for prolonged periods? Ask more questions.

3. Free play is crucial. A good preschool weaves plenty of it into the school day.

4. Look for preschools that are thinking, talking, and developing classroom practices around enhancing the so-called soft skills in students—ones that set the stage for school success.

CHAPTER TWO

TESTING

> One almost might say, "It matters very little what the
> tests are so long as they are numerous."
> —ALFRED BINET (1857–1911)

THE THIRD GRADERS at Tyler Heights Elementary
School in Annapolis, Maryland, were nervous before they sat down
to take the state's annual high-stakes test, the Maryland School
Assessment. In the weeks leading up to it, the teachers there had
taken every step possible to make sure the children were taking the
tests seriously. There were practice tests, pep rallies, posters, even
meditation sessions to help the children use their chi to get top
grades. But the morning of the big test, those eight- and nine-year-
olds were still quaking with anxiety. "They knew the tests mattered
but many of them believed they would be held back if they didn't do
well, which wasn't exactly true," said Linda Perlstein, a newspaper
reporter who later went on to write *Tested: One American School
Struggles to Make the Grade*, about the school's effort to improve

their high-stakes test scores. What was true was that the test would have a huge impact on how their school was run. At Tyler Heights, like nearly all public schools around the nation, school administrators who operate schools where pupils score well get more autonomy to conduct their programs. Schools where children's scores are sliding face sanctions—sometimes harsh ones. In New York City, for instance, schools are given letter grades based in part on test scores, and the letter grades are published in the newspaper. In the city of Oakland, the testing data is condensed and schools are assigned an overall number that is meant to measure the school's effectiveness in educating kids. In most districts across the country, schools where children are not scoring well are being reorganized. Some are being closed.

Tests matter outside of education circles also. Home owners in every middle-class community keep tabs on whether tests scores are rising or falling. In this difficult economy, house prices depend on it. Real estate agents can demand a premium for property that is in the "best" school district. When parents are considering bidding on a new family home, they look immediately at test scores. "We were relocating from Chicago," says Sarah Tierney, who lives in a suburb in Douglas County, Colorado, where her two sons, Matthew, seven, and Ryan, eleven, attend public school, "and when the real estate agent made the pitch that Douglas County schools were tops, I checked the scores on the Internet. And we bought a house there." Test grades carry political clout: increasingly, elected officials use it as a yardstick to measure the efficiency of their management. When New York City mayor Michael Bloomberg ran for reelection in 2009, he boasted of state test scores that showed two-thirds of city students were passing English and 82 percent were passing math. (He won by a large margin, but later those gains in test scores turned out to be largely illusory.) Education is a sprawling, complicated enterprise, but for many of us looking for a good school for our children, scores on standardized tests have become the bottom line.

It's big business, too. Right now, testing for public schools, college admissions, and professional certifications and degrees is about a $2 billion industry. In Iowa City, Iowa, population 67,000, the two main employers in the community are test behemoths ACT and Pearson. Amid the cornfields that surround the city are massive climate-controlled warehouses where three-foot-high stacks of answer sheets sit on steel dollies, ready to be fed assembly-line-style into automatic scoring machines.

It can seem like standardized tests have become the tail that wags the dog. As it did in Tyler Heights, preparing for tests can dominate the school year. In some schools, children spend five or six weeks—and in other schools even more—prepping or taking standardized state tests, county tests, district tests, and school-wide tests. And that doesn't even take into account teacher-devised tests to measure how well a child is doing, say, in social studies. "We just don't have room in the schedule to add one more test," a principal told me recently. Principals and teachers are tying themselves into Gordian knots trying to instruct, support, cajole, and badger kids into performing at the peak of their ability on tests.

There are plenty of people who believe that standardized tests are bad for our schools. They believe that there are better measures of achievement—a child should give a presentation on the root causes of the American Civil War, for instance, or participate in a debate over slavery—rather than taking a fill-in-the-bubble-type exam along with every other kid in the state. We shouldn't ignore their arguments—they may be lighting the path for where schools of the future will need to go. As I write this, the new federal education initiative Race to the Top is giving consortiums of states the money to come up with more innovative ways to assess learning. But let's stay with today's reality. Right now in the United States, all educational stakeholders—parents, kids, teachers, administrators, policy makers, and politicians—use testing data to measure the health of our schools. This process is codified in federal and state law. For the time being, tests are here to stay.

So, do test scores matter? Sure. You cannot ignore them when you are thinking about where to send your child to school. But you should also know what test experts know: making a decision about whether to send your child to a school based solely on test scores is a little like deciding which car to buy based on the color of the paint. There are other measures to weigh if you want to make a good decision. This chapter will help you figure out what tests really measure, what they say about the school, and the short-term upside and long-term downside of "teaching to the test." Some schools with high test scores are doing a fantastic job. Other schools with high test scores are cheating their students out of a good education. This chapter will show you how to tell the difference.

THE MEASURE OF THE MAN

It's safe to say that no one likes to test more than Americans do. Throughout the nineteenth and twentieth centuries, testing experts from various disciplines had a field day coming up with ways to sort people by intelligence, moral fiber, criminal leanings, and personality traits. Testing experts claimed to be able to predict things about your aptitude and appetites based on the lumps on your head, the shape of your face, the shape of your brain, the weight of pieces of your brain, your interpretation of random-seeming drawings, and your answers to ambiguous and open-ended questions. Intelligence tests, the so-called IQ exam, were adapted from the humanitarian ideas of French psychologist Alfred Binet and were, for a time, regarded as a scientific tool for sorting superior citizens from defective ones. They've been used—and abused—from 1914 to this very day.

Our obsession with testing in schools began and reached full flower with the Scholastic Aptitude Test. First unveiled in 1926, the SAT was designed to precisely calibrate the intangible qualities that a child needed to succeed in higher education. A child's score on the SAT, test takers were told, was a dependable indicator of whether a child had the right stuff to enter the Ivory Tower or was better equipped for more humble pursuits. You couldn't study for it. It measured aptitude, something either you had or you didn't.

The SAT was a perfect sorting instrument for its time. The subsection of kids that colleges wanted—affluent and middle-class white males—did best on the SATs. Girls trailed. Working-class and poor kids and boys and girls of color brought up the rear. As for predicting aptitude? Numerous studies have shown that the SAT score can explain about 16 percent of the variation in a student's freshman grades. Looking for the best predictor of performance in the first year of college? A student's high school record. The SAT combined with high school grades adds only modestly to the predictive powers of the high school grades alone. These days, the College Board, which administers the SAT, has dropped *aptitude* out of the name and acknowledges that it tests a certain body of information. The more of that knowledge you have, they claim, the better equipped you are to handle college-level work. On their Web site, they concede that it's possible—even desirable—to study for it.

SAT test prep companies do the College Board one better. Courses like Kaplan and Princeton Review boast that a ten-week course will raise your score 100 points overall—or your money back. The more intensive the course, the more you pay and, presumably, the better you can do on the test. Gaming the SAT is a $960-million-a-year business all its own.

In public schools, children have been taking standardized tests for decades. For years, states administered exams with names like the Iowa Tests of Basic Skills and Stanford Achievement Test and the TerraNova (formerly the California Test of Basic Skills). Teachers didn't prepare for those tests. In fact, no one even cared what was on them. Children didn't pass or fail them. Schools did not live and die by the outcome. The testing developer selected a model group of kids, then developed a test in a way so that a small number of those model kids scored poorly, a big group scored in the middle, and a small number scored very well indeed. Later, when regular schoolchildren took the test, their scores were measured against the scores of the model kids. Schoolchildren didn't pass or fail the Iowa Tests of Basic Skills. Instead, they were given a percentile rank—as in "Congratulations! You scored in the 86th percentile"—which, if they cared, meant they scored better than 85 percent of those model kids who helped test developers cook up the exam in the first place.

Those exams functioned a bit like a satellite—providing state education officials and lawmakers with a crude portrait of how effectively the education system in their state was operating. When it came time to draw up budgets, policy makers looked at test scores to give them a rough idea of which schools needed to get programs beefed up and how they might expend taxpayer dollars to improve overall levels of education.

As the accountability movement picked up speed in the 1980s and 1990s, states began designing and administering their own standardized tests—with the goal of getting schools to teach roughly the same curriculum and to garner more data on the performance of individual schools. During the Clinton administration, the federal government demanded that states test kids in reading and math at least once in elementary school, once in middle school, and once in high school. In 2001, the federal No Child Left Behind statute wrote that patchwork state-by-state effort into a single, broad, national law.

The controversial statute had two provisions. The first one required states to come up with a set of educational standards—topics, concepts, and skills in reading and math—that schoolkids would be expected to know at each grade level. Parents from middle-class and wealthy districts, in general, have found it hard to accept this provision of the law. Their teachers, they believed, were already providing kids with a rich curriculum. State standards often seemed simplistic by comparison. In less effective schools, which were often in poor neighborhoods, parents were more open to the idea of statewide standards: those parents hoped that state standards would challenge teachers in underperforming schools to up their game.

The second requirement of the No Child Left Behind law was that all children were to be tested in reading and math in grades three through eight. Critics pointed out that those requirements ignored a solid two-thirds of what happens in a school day, including social studies, science, art, history, and music. Supporters argued that it was about time states were charged with measuring the progress of kids who had long been ignored—English-language learners, kids who were in special education, and poor African American kids.

This testing had to be done quickly and cheaply, so states opted for the kind of fill-in-the-bubble exams like the Iowa Tests of Basic Skills that had worked so well in years past. This time around, though, there were no model kids against which to measure the scores. Instead, states determined what score was good enough by setting what became known as the cut score. If all the subgroups of kids were moving toward the cut score, the school was considered to be doing well. If some subgroups lagged, say, special education kids, and didn't improve over the course of several years, the school was labeled "in need of improvement" and was sanctioned. Counties, districts, and schools began administering—twice yearly, seasonally, and sometimes every six weeks—standardized tests of their own in order to predict the outcomes of those all-important state tests. These days, it seems, filling in the bubbles on multiple-choice standardized tests has become as much a part of schooling as clapping chalk dust out of erasers was when our parents went to school.

BUBBLE MADNESS

So what goes on when a child takes a standardized test? The answer might surprise you. Say, hypothetically, that your state's seventh-grade reading curriculum standards, like many around the country, include teaching kids to be able to tell the difference between literary texts (such as fiction, poetry, and biographies) and informational texts (such as documents, persuasive texts, and the manual that came with your latest MP3 player).

In the best possible world, your child's teacher is familiar with the standard and spends about a week instructing kids on the difference between these two forms of writing in a clear and accessible manner. In the same world, the hypothetical students are not throwing spitballs, texting, or daydreaming about Justin Bieber, but paying rapt attention. They finish the week with a newfound understanding of the difference between those two kinds of writing.

We are talking about the best possible world, but we are still talking about the world. The teachers in it are variable and kids even more so. As in any classroom, some students will have a highly sophisticated understanding of the distinctions, some will understand them pretty well, and others (most likely the ones who were texting and daydreaming) will have just the vaguest notion of what the teacher was talking about. Even in the classrooms where the very best teachers teach the very smartest kids, all of them aren't going to end up grasping the material at exactly the same level. Schools are made up of people, not robots.

Now let's take a closer look at the test itself. We'd imagine that a hypothetical test designed to measure whether kids understand the hypothetical curriculum (in this case, the difference between literary and informational writing) would require children to answer a series of questions. Since policy makers want to keep the test brief so that it is easy and inexpensive to score, maybe they'll choose three. What do those questions consist of? Here's one approach: the first would require the most basic understanding of the material in order to answer correctly, the second, a slightly more sophisticated understanding, and the final, a question that requires a rich understanding of the differences between those two forms in order to answer correctly. With this kind of test, each answer the child provides helps determine a two-pronged question: Do these seventh graders know the difference between literary and informational writing? And how well do they know it?

But if you guessed that this is what a state's high-stakes test for seventh-grade reading looks like, you'd be wrong. Let's walk through what actually goes on. I suspect it might change the way you look at testing scores forever.

WHAT IS A STANDARDIZED TEST, ANYWAY?

When the state education authorities want to know if your child knows a particular standard, in this case, whether your child can tell the difference between literary and informational writing, they hire a group of test assessment professionals—mostly researchers and statisticians with a background in education. Those test builders use chunks of the material covered in the standards (in the case of our hypothetical, the difference between literary and informational writing) to fashion their questions. But the question or questions will never be able to test the depth of kids' knowledge on those two forms of writing in the way that you might expect. Test builders design questions about literary and informational writing with one aim: to have roughly 40 to 60 percent of the students answer correctly. When they get those results, the test builders believe that the test question is a legitimate proxy for the material the kids learned. Why this quirky criteria? According to their statistical models, somewhere between 40 and 60 percent of the kids are likely to understand any given material. So when they ask a question and about 40 to 60 percent of the kids get it right, then voilà! It is considered, in the land of standardized testing, a legitimate, statistically defensible question. Remember our proposed model—with an easy, middling, and hard question? Here's why it won't work. If the question is asked in such a way that 100 percent of the kids get the right answer, then that question is no good. It doesn't reflect the distribution of ability that experts can show exists in a classroom. A really hard test question—one that could only be answered by students who understand the richest and most complex part of the material— would never appear on a standardized test. Why? It's not what standardized tests do. Remember: the goal of each standardized test question is not to assess what the smartest kids know but to create again and again a statistically defensible pattern of answers for each question.

As parents, we sometimes ask kids questions that we are sure they either know or don't know because we are probing the limits of their understanding. If we ask them questions that are too easy (Honey, did you know you have to put the clear bag in the recycle container?), their response, especially if they are in middle school, will be a snort and an eye roll but also confirmation for us that they have picked up some important bit of information about the world. If we ask them a question that is too hard (Do you have enough gas in your car to pick up all four friends and make the hundred-mile drive both to and from the concert?), and they can't come up with a good answer, we know, at least, that we've got them thinking about the issue. In classrooms, good teachers work in much the same way—continually checking in with students to make sure they've got the material or circling back to reteach it until the kids do comprehend it. The world of standardized test design is very different. For test designers, questions that all the kids get right or wrong are called statistical "noise"—and are to be avoided.

To get these statistically juicy answers (juicy, at least, by standardized testing standards), the test makers pull material from the lower-middle range of what they know most kids can do. Remember—they want 40 to 60 percent of the kids to get them right so the question has to be culled from what would be the middling level of understanding. And that's where the trouble comes in.

WHAT'S WRONG WITH TEACHING TO THE TEST?

For as long as there have been standardized tests, there have been people who've bitterly complained about instructors who teach to the test. But let's ask ourselves: What's wrong with that? I learned about the ancient Greeks in fifth grade. My teacher outlined his curriculum and then gave us a test at the end of the year that consisted of harder and harder questions about those democracy-and-toga-loving people. Some of us did well, others of us, less well. When No Child Left Behind became the law, it seemed that the biggest change was that my fifth-grade history teacher was told that he had to teach to the state standard, which turned out to be a lot of information about, you guessed it, ancient Greeks. And teaching to the test? Well, at first pass, that kind of made sense. If a fifth grader is going to have to sit for state-mandated tests on ancient Greeks, then by all means, teach the material that he'll be tested on.

But once you know how standardized tests are constructed, teaching to the test starts to seem like a very bad idea indeed. Standardized test questions are being pulled from the lower part of the middle range of what kids can do. If teachers at a school are encouraged to "teach to the test," they can probably show you test scores that are going up, but it means they are focusing their instruction on the most basic part of the material. And that's not a particularly ambitious goal for a classroom or a school.

The other, even more subtle problem with teaching to the test is that prepping the kids for testing disrupts what should be the natural distribution of correct answers. If the teacher teaches to the test, all the kids might answer the question correctly. But remember, answering the question itself was not the point—it was just a small chunk of course material acting as a proxy for a bigger chunk of course material. And if a teacher successfully gets all kids to answer a test question correctly, it moves from a good, valid question to being statistical "noise." That doesn't stop schools from encouraging teachers to shape their instruction around getting kids to pass the test. Social scientists say it's almost inevitable. The phenomenon even has a name: it's called Campbell's law, after a famous (in his world) psychologist named Donald T. Campbell. His law states that "the more any quantitative social indicator is used for social decision-making, the more subject it will be to corruption pressures and the more apt it will be to distort and corrupt the social processes it is intended to monitor." There are educational consulting companies who are only too happy to speed along the corruption process. They sell—and many districts buy—lesson plans and teacher guides to help teachers teach to the test.

John Tanner is a testing expert who spent the last fifteen years working with big test companies, at both the Delaware Department of Education and, later, a Washington, D.C., think tank. He draws a parallel between encouraging or even allowing teachers to teach to the test, and encouraging people to study for the eye test before they go to the DMV. "What would happen," Tanner says, "is that we'd have a lot of people passing the test but not have a clue whether they can actually see well enough to drive. If schools feeling the pressure of test-based accountability anticipate the tested material in any way, then the real truth is we won't have a clue from the results whether or not kids are being properly educated. We'll have lots of numbers and test scores and accountability calculations that we can pretend mean something that they in fact do not, and they'll look believable so we may do just that. But believing won't transform them into something more useful."

Tanner runs a company called Test Sense, which explains to school officials what I've just described to you. Then he tries to get those same officials to amp up the curriculum so that the lower middle level of material—which will keep scores up—is embedded in a rich, deep curriculum. It's a difficult business. Administrators know their jobs are on the line—and the desire for a quick fix is overwhelming. But there is another factor that makes Tanner's job difficult: no one really wants to believe that standardized tests—which promise to translate this sprawling complicated thing called education into numerical precision—are really that limited, or that limiting. Tanner worries that parents see rising test scores and assume that schools are doing fine. And that's a mistake. "Like the compromised eye-test, by the time we recognize the results have failed to answer the question it is too late—students will have passed by our sphere of influence and drivers who badly need glasses will have been the cause of more wrecks than we care to imagine. For more and more of our students, it's getting closer and closer to being too late. For many of them it already is."

Instead of being falsely confident that scores on standardized tests are a simple code that measures whether enough learning is taking place in a school, we need to view test scores like a financial statement—and examine them with the same blend of critical thinking, curiosity, and common sense we'd harness before we'd invest our nest egg. Yes, the Alpha Corporation may appear to be in an enviable position: they dominate the market share, have plenty of customers looking to buy their product, and also seem to be awash in cash. Ready to invest? Maybe ask a few more questions. How did they get to this spot? Are they awash in cash because they recently fired all their employees? Have they purchased enough raw materials to make good on the orders they've taken? Or are they bolstering the bottom line at the expense of long-term gains?

This discussion about testing is sometimes hard to grasp. And even the testing gurus like Daniel Koretz, a professor of education at Harvard and author of *Measuring Up: What Educational Testing Really Tells Us*, one of the best books on the subject, cautions that it is incredibly hard to distinguish between real and bogus gains in scores. But before you get too frustrated, I'm going to provide you with the four Silver Bullet Questions that test designers say you should ask when you are looking at test scores.

1. Ask to see scores broken out by subgroups. A mean test score—even if it is rising—means almost nothing. Really. Nobody who knows statistics would find a mean score for an entire grade of students meaningful.

2. Make sure you look at long-term trends. A one-year test score change, even when it is going up, also means next to nothing.

3. Scores (not means) for subgroups still rising over the long term? Great. Now it is time to find out what's creating that upward trend. Ask the principal these two questions: What are the three decisions that you've made in the last two years in an effort to impact student achievement in your school? What are the results?

4. Still want to get a better measure of the school? Ask this: What is your intervention plan for the lower-quartile students—the bottom of the class? And how are you progressing with that plan? Even if your kids are not in the lowest quartile, this matters to you. If the school has a solid plan for hard-to-teach kids, they are likely to have a solid plan for your kid, too.

Remember, good test scores won't tell you if the teachers at that school are doing a great job, working hard to impart a deep, rich, complex, and meaningful curriculum, or if they are subjecting students to dumbed-down material to improve results without truly improving learning. Students in both kinds of classrooms can get the answers on a standardized test correct. But kids in the former class have engaged in real learning. And kids in the latter have been deprived of real learning to make the school look good.

THE TAKE AWAYS

1. Standardized test results are only a single measure of a school's success. It measures about a third of the curriculum that is taught in a school. Do not rely solely on test scores to evaluate a school.

2. Drop the contest mentality. It's infectious but it is also pointless. The truth is this: one year of mean test scores is meaningless. You don't need an Excel spreadsheet but you do need to look at scores from subgroups of kids over a period of years to get an accurate picture of what's going on in the school.

3. If school administrators easily and breezily equate "We have good test scores" with "We're doing a good job"— beware. Some people in these positions don't actually understand the limits of what those test scores are measuring. Some do, and are counting on the fact that you won't.

CHAPTER THREE

CLASS SIZE

Smaller classes are not the only answer, but they are an indispensable part of the solution to the crisis facing Florida's public schools.

—FROM PEOPLE FOR THE AMERICAN WAY,
AN ADVOCACY GROUP THAT SUPPORTS
SMALL CLASS SIZES

FEW THINGS ABOUT a school seem to matter more to parents than class size. For many of us it is the litmus test for a well-run school. Small class size speaks of a school that is focused on putting resources in the right place—not administrative retreats, paneling for the principal's office, or expensive but rarely used classroom technology. Small class size is a signal to us that a hundred smaller decisions that accompany the running of a school have been shaped with our children as a priority. As a result, a school is able to invest in an appropriate number of teachers.

Classrooms with fifteen students and one teacher usually look better, too—more controlled than classrooms with thirty kids. At best, we imagine that small classes are environments where our children will be closely observed and where teachers have the opportunity to get to know each child. We assume that in small classes our children will receive personalized attention and that learning can be sprinkled like stardust through the thoughtful, free-ranging give-and-take between student and teacher. Small class size creates an environment that invites parent involvement, as well. If your daughter is one of thirty second-graders, you know without being told that the teacher is going to be hard-pressed to remember which reading group your daughter is in, much less her progress with phonemes.

It's not surprising that so many parents will move heaven and earth to get their children in schools with a low teacher-student ratio.

When Rhona Hartwick, who lives in a suburb outside of Denver, toured elementary schools for her son, Marc, who was entering kindergarten, class size was foremost in her mind. A popular charter she'd heard about from other moms turned out to be a bust—the atmosphere was chaotic and one first-grade classroom had twenty-seven kids it in. "Too many," she declared.

She liked many things about her neighborhood elementary school—the building was new, the outdoor space was ample, clean, and inviting, the principal seemed on the ball. But when she walked into a second-grade classroom, her heart sank. She counted twenty-four children and a single teacher. "The classroom was running smoothly when I was there but I wondered what would happen when something unexpected came up—a child who needed extra help, a discipline problem. Frankly, I wanted to do a little better for our son."

PEG TYRE

A week later, she toured a private school that was a forty-minute drive from her home. In second grade there were twenty children. "It seemed, I don't know, cozier. With twenty children, the teacher could give each one plenty of attention." That night, she sat at the kitchen table with her husband, Marc Sr., who designs heating and air-conditioning systems for shopping malls. They took out a calculator, trying to make the numbers work. "The private school tuition was just out of our reach," says Rhona. "Any way I added up the numbers, I couldn't find a way to stretch our budget to cover it. My husband and I had talked about having more children, of someday moving to a better neighborhood, but that night, I was thinking maybe I should return to work."

The extra income she could bring in, she thought, could buy her son a better education.

The Hartwicks were ready to make some big sacrifices to enroll their son in a school that had small classes.

Does it really matter? For the Hartwicks, the answer was yes. But you may be surprised to learn that the effects of class size on learning are not 100 percent clear. Conventional wisdom tell us that smaller class size is crucial for learning—that kids of all ages learn more in smaller groups. And indeed, in the early years of schooling, there is some research to back this up.

But there is a substantial body of research to suggest that kids in small classes don't necessarily learn more. In the range of things that schools can do to improve outcomes for your child, reducing class size may rank a distant fourth behind solid teacher training, a clear and well-sequenced curriculum, and a staff that is well supported and regularly evaluated. (You'll read more about the last two elements in chapters 4, 5, and 7.)

For decades, class size was largely a function of a community's

74

population. A lot of kids born in a particular year? The local school found a way to cram them into classrooms. In the 1970s, though, as the discussion of the achievement gap sharpened and schools began to be seen as an instrument of racial oppression, "overcrowding" became a catchall concept for the inequities between poor and middle-class kids in public education. Writers like liberal activist Jonathan Kozol decried the antiquated, crumbling, and overcrowded classrooms where poor children had their dreams denied. "The overcrowded classroom" was associated with poor performance, high truancy, and high rates of juvenile crime.

In the last twenty years, legislators have tried to institute statewide standards in an effort to keep teacher-student ratios low, especially in poor and underperforming schools. Currently, thirty-two states now set aside funds for a voluntary or mandatory reduction in class size. These policies have had a substantial effect. In the last ten years, class size in America has declined—and continues to drop. According to the National Center for Education Statistics, the average class size of U.S. elementary schools has been reduced from twenty-four pupils in 1993 to twenty pupils in 2007.

Currently, not all poor kids are in overcrowded classes. In schools that serve rural poor kids, for instance, class sizes tend to be small. Urban schools that serve impoverished kids tend to be larger than their more affluent suburban counterparts, though. In public schools in inner-city Chicago, for example, kindergarten through eighth-grade classrooms are 14 percent larger than the average-size classrooms throughout Illinois (and considerably larger than the teacher-student ratio in schools in the affluent suburbs that ring the city). In New York City, fourth-grade and eighth-grade classroom sizes are 10 percent and 17 percent higher, respectively, than the average classroom size in the rest of the state.

Right now, the discussion about class size is a polarized and highly political one. Fiscal conservatives and corporate management–style reformers who have been enjoying center stage in so many recent education debates say that smaller class size is simply too darn expensive for what turns out to be very minor improvements in student achievement. And it comes at a huge cost. Florida alone has spent nearly $20 billion reducing class size after the number of students per classroom was capped in 2003.

In these difficult financial times, as states struggle to balance their budgets, state officials say they need to be more strategic with their dollars and to fund programs that show a greater and more consistent improvement for a wide swath of kids. They suggest that parents are manipulated by teachers unions into wanting small classrooms because it takes the scrutiny off the effectiveness of their rank and file.

Michelle Rhee, the former chancellor of schools for the District of Columbia, now heads the advocacy group Students First. Not long ago, she told a group of reporters that with the right preparation, bigger classes, not smaller ones, would be an effective way to raise test scores and save money. "The way that I think would make sense is to identify the most highly effective teachers in a particular district, and think about assigning a few more students to each of their classrooms," Rhee says. Those same fiscal conservatives and corporate-style school managers accuse the teachers unions of pushing the small-is-good agenda to the detriment of kids.

In general, the powerful teachers unions do endorse small class size. Although it is popular to bash the unions, you can look at their enthusiasm for small class size in a couple of different ways. It may be an honest reflection of the experience of the people who are on the front lines in education. A great number of classroom teachers point out that they can barely learn the names of thirty students by the end of the first month of school, much less pitch instruction to different learning styles so the students can learn best. Teachers also describe a sense of connectedness that can grow in a small class, creating a learning environment that is intimate, flexible, and, when it works, highly productive. A more cynical take is that the union support for small classrooms is part of an effort to protect the working conditions of its members. Smaller class size makes it easier for teachers to teach. It takes much less time to grade fifteen essays than thirty.

The most cynical take is that smaller class size also increases the number of teachers who are hired and strengthens the union that supports them. Randi Weingarten, head of the American Federation of Teachers, acknowledges that raising class size is a branch on a tree of hard decisions that cash-strapped states are facing. But, she says, "if somebody says they want to raise class size, they're doing it because they want to cut the budget, not because it's actually going to help children." Teachers' union representatives point out that the same fiscal conservatives and corporate-type reformers who encourage high student-to-teacher ratios in classrooms are often the ones who send their own children to private schools where—you guessed it—the kids receive instruction in small groups, often twelve to fifteen in a class.

At this point, it is tempting to bury your face in your hands. Like so many issues in education, there is no single "truth" about small class size that you can fit on a bumper sticker. *Don't despair.* It is an important question. In this chapter, we're going to pick apart some of the research on small class size and see what conclusions can be drawn from it and what might be useful to your family.

Does class size matter? For some interesting reasons, it's hard for researchers to come up with a definitive answer. A group of analysts followed children over time and correlated the size of the class they were assigned to with how much they learned. Ordinarily, these would be juicy studies, but how kids ended up in classes with small teacher-student ratios created some confounding factors. Children who attended elementary school in affluent Wilmette, Illinois, for example, may have been educated in classes that had fifteen kids and one teacher and showed huge gains in their academic achievement compared to kids in larger classes in nearby inner-city Chicago. But was it the class size or the opportunities that went along with privilege that made the difference?

Doug Ready, an education sociologist from Teachers College at Columbia University in New York, points out that schools with class sizes that are small by default are different in many ways—and provide different outcomes—from those that provide smaller classes by design. But even when school administrators purposefully create small classes and researchers explore the learning outcomes, the results need to be taken with a grain of salt. Principals create smaller classes for a variety of reasons. They can assign tough-to-teach kids to smaller classes, or they can create smaller classes for their weakest or inexperienced teachers. In both these cases, graphs and charts of what the students learn are likely to reflect outcomes that depend on many factors that won't necessarily apply to your child's school or your community.

Then there are studies that involve a large, nationally representative sample of children—the same proportion of affluent and less-affluent kids that would be found in public schools around the nation—which are a bit more revealing. In this chapter, we'll consider two of the most prominent studies from the Early Childhood Longitudinal Study, Kindergarten class of 1998–99 (known in sociology circles by the catchy nickname ECLS-K). Those two studies assessed the learning of twenty thousand kids who were in kindergarten and first grade during the 1998–99 school year. One study, which looked at the kids who attended public and private schools, found that small class size had no effect on student learning in reading or mathematics. The other study, which used the same data set minus the private-school kids, found that kindergarten and first-grade children who attended classes that were seventeen kids and one teacher or less learned about three weeks more than kindergartners and first graders who learned in large groups—greater than twenty-five students. In that study, kids in middle-size classrooms—between eighteen and twenty-five kids per teacher—also did slightly better than the kids in the very big classrooms.

What we learn is that all things being equal, big classes aren't ideal—medium and small-size ones are better. It seems that in smaller classes teachers are able to teach more. But the differential between kids who attend big ones and kids who attend small ones amounts to only three weeks of learning per year—a surprisingly small margin.

Other more formally designed experiments in class size provide us with further clues as to who may benefit from smaller classes. In 1985, researchers in the state of Tennessee randomly assigned over six thousand kindergartners to one of three experimental conditions: (a) a small class of between thirteen and seventeen kids and a single teacher, (b) a large class with twenty-two to twenty-six children and a single teacher, and (c) a large class of twenty-two to twenty-six children led by a teacher and an aide. At the end of kindergarten, the achievement of the children in small classes was almost a month ahead of the achievement of the kids in the other two kinds of classes. By the end of first grade, the kids in the small class were almost two months ahead. After four years, children in small classes were 5.4 months ahead in reading and 3.1 months ahead in mathematics. In small classes, kids learned more. So in that way, small classes were successful.

But the way some education researchers look at it, this experiment showed that small class size was a big disappointment. Why? I would like my kids to learn as much as they possibly can each school year. But the Holy Grail of educational intervention is a little more ambitious. Researchers are constantly looking for interventions that improve the rate of learning. Small class size doesn't do it. Every year kids who were in smaller classes learned about a month more than kids in larger classes—which means if they got smaller classes for three years, they'd be three months ahead of kids from the large classes. But the rate at which they learned was never compounding—smaller classes gave students the equivalent of an extra month every time. The personal attention didn't kick-start their ability to learn any faster.

Which doesn't mean it's not worth doing. It means that small class size alone is not going to help underachieving kids catch up and stay on par with high achievers. And even though the rate of learning did not continue to accelerate, the positive effects of small class size were long-lasting. When the kids who were assigned to small classes in kindergarten through third grade got to high school, they were earning higher grades and were more likely to complete advanced academic classes, take college admissions tests, and graduate.

Later analysis of this data, and additional data from a 1996 study of small class size in low-income schools in Wisconsin, highlights an interesting point: African American kids who attended predominantly African American schools get a bigger boost from small class size than did white kids. In Tennessee, on average, black students in small classes ended third grade with academic achievement that was 7 to 10 percentage points higher than black students who attended the large classes. White students in small classes were only 3 to 5 percentage points ahead of white students from those larger classes.

Before you pull out your cell phone, ask to speak to your child's principal, and demand that your precious gem gets moved into a smaller class, let's reflect a bit about what this research means. The best study we have finds a small but persistent difference when you compare kids in a classroom of twelve to seventeen kids to a classroom with twenty-two to twenty-six. If you are making big decisions about your family life and your child's education to get your child moved from a twenty-four-child classroom to one with twenty children in it, you may be acting on your best instinct, but the research doesn't necessarily back you up.

The Tennessee study has become the gold standard in most debates about class size. It has also come under a lot of fire. Researchers who revisited the schools where the study was conducted suggested that some parents may have advocated to get their kids in the smaller classes—thus making the "random" part of the study not so random. Others pointed out that some kids were in big classes and then transferred to smaller ones—and those tended to be the kids of activist parents, the same parents who would make sure their children got their homework done. Researchers also complained that certain protocols that should have been in place were faulty. For the results to be considered "pure," for example, none of the test subjects should know which of them is getting active treatment and which is getting a placebo. In the Tennessee study, teachers were told that they were taking part in a test to determine the effect of small classes on learning, and that might have, consciously or unconsciously, affected the way they taught.

To be sure, all the nay-saying and bellyaching about the way the Tennessee test was conducted didn't slow the enthusiasm of class-size-reduction proponents. In fact, the Tennessee project changed education policy in the entire state of California. In 1996, state education officials on the West Coast got legislators to appropriate

$1 billion a year to cap elementary school class sizes at a strict twenty kids to one teacher. A pricy undertaking, it led to an unprecedented hiring binge, with the state bringing 28,886 new teachers on board.

Six years later, the Rand Corporation published a study examining the results of the California effort—and it was discouraging. The good news was that, overall, California's educational performance had gone up. The bad news was this: despite hiring all those new teachers, the kids in the small classes were performing about the same as kids in the larger classes. And those positive downstream effects—better grades in high school and higher graduation rates—never materialized, either.

So, what happened? No one is sure. But there are two strong hypotheses: either the Tennessee results were specific to that state and that experiment, or—and this is one that most educational experts favor—teacher quality matters more than class size. California went on a hiring spree at a time when there were not a lot of highly qualified teachers waiting around on the sidelines to be hired. Because they had to hire so many teachers so quickly, they paid little attention to hiring the best ones. While very small classes early on seem to provide an advantage for kids—particularly low-income African American kids—good teachers, it seems, are even more important for increasing student achievement.

MIDDLE SCHOOL YEARS

While much of the robust research on class size has been focused on the early years, parents continue to weigh the value of small class size in those sometimes tricky later years of elementary school and middle school. Kids become more social. Learning deficits, which may have been hidden in the early years, need to be addressed. Early puberty hits some kids very hard. Parents are right to be concerned about these years—when you parse the data on who graduates from high school and who doesn't, the dispirited slump of a soon-to-be high school dropout often begins long before your sophomore stops showing up for math class and then for school altogether. Difficulties at school often blossom in the late elementary school years and fester through middle school. People who study graduation rate know that for at-risk kids, ninth grade is the make-or-break year.

So what does the research say about small class sizes in late elementary and middle school years? Unless you are talking about dramatically smaller classes, say, moving a kid from a class of thirty to a class of fifteen, it doesn't seem to make a whole lot of difference to his or her academics. But there are other factors to consider aside from academics. Thomas Dee, an economist at Swarthmore, and Martin West, a professor at the Harvard Graduate School of Education, conducted an interesting study on the effect of class size on those more subtle factors that are so meaningful to parents—namely, engagement, motivation, and self-discipline.

For years, these were issues parents talked about but social scientists ignored—how to help kids become motivated, engaged, and hardworking, and to be able to plan for big projects. As we discussed in the preschool chapter, social scientists have been taking a closer look at the role of those so-called soft skills. The research community is now becoming aware that being "good at school" helps kids learn.

In 2008, Dee and West went back and looked at that old data from the Reagan-era Tennessee study. After conducting mathematical gymnastics to overcome some of the methodological problems with the study, Dee and West found that, on the whole, kids who were assigned to small classes in the early years had only a small increase in those positive, noncognitive skills and that even that small increase didn't last. When those kids were tested again in eighth grade, there was pretty much no difference in their noncognitive skills.

Not content with that finding, the economists then looked at the National Education Longitudinal Study. Since 1988, researchers have been collecting information on a nationally representative sample of 24,599 eighth-grade students from over 1,000 schools. In the section of the data that Dee and West were examining, students came from about 815 public schools, with about 26 students from each of those schools. The data consisted of class assignment, performance, and a three-question survey from students: (a) Is this subject useful? (b) Do you look forward to it? and (c) Are you afraid to ask questions?

Two of each student's academic teachers (i.e., a math or science teacher and an English or history teacher) also answered questions about the student and provided information about their certification, education, and experience and the size of their sampled classes.

Dee and West found that eighth graders in smaller classes were more engaged, particularly in urban schools. And interestingly, teachers who were heading up smaller classes tended to respond to certain kinds of students differently. In nationwide surveys, teachers report that boys pay less attention than girls. Nationally, more Hispanics tend to be identified as disruptive than adolescents of European descent. Teachers who headed up smaller classes had significantly less of a problem with these two groups of kids.

While Dee and West's study may not cause a state policy maker to recast an education budget, it may be significant to parents. We know that some children will be able to thrive in many kinds of educational environments. Some are more sensitive. Some children enter adolescence and become oppositional and disengaged. For middle schoolers in the last two categories, who are wobbling socially or academically, finding a school that can provide smaller class size may be worth the effort.

THE TAKE AWAYS

1. The ideal class size for elementary school students is probably thirteen to seventeen kids. There doesn't seem to be a difference between a classroom of twenty-five kids, for instance, and a classroom of twenty kids.

2. Classes with over twenty-five kids are not optimal. Adding a paraprofessional to help the teacher might make the classroom run more smoothly but doesn't seem to improve outcomes for students.

3. In general, a highly effective teacher is probably better for your child than is a small class.

4. There is not much research to suggest that older kids do better academically in smaller classes, though there is some research to suggest that smaller classes in eighth grade promote more engagement in learning and less friction between teacher and student.

CHAPTER FOUR

READING: WHAT IT TAKES TO SUCCEED

Polonius: "What do you read, My Lord?"
Hamlet: "Words, Words, Words."

HAMLET, ACT II, SCENE II

SOME TIME, USUALLY between the ages of five and six, most children begin to read. Watching a child transition from a nonreader to one who can both entertain and educate herself with a book is, for many parents, one of the milestones and miracles of family life.

Learning to read accurately, fluidly, with good comprehension and stamina, is also a crucial set of skills for school success. Schools know this. That's why in the best ones, the early years of primary education are devoted to teaching kids to read using scientifically proven methods to ensure that all kids are reading at grade level.

But in many schools in all kinds of neighborhoods there is a shockingly large chunk of kids—about one in three—who don't master the skills they need to learn to read in a sophisticated way. Their road is a difficult one: although many will try to use their intelligence to cover the holes in their skill set, as the work gets harder and the reading grows more complex, these children will find they are unable to keep up.

This is one of the great tragedies of the American school system. It is even more heartbreaking when you talk to scientists about how the human brain reads. Researchers estimate that somewhere between 2 and 5 percent of children, most of whom have developmental disorders or profound neurological problems, will never learn to read. The rest? If they are given what experts say is the right kind of instruction, they will learn to read, and most of them will be able to read well.

This chapter will familiarize you with the kind of instruction all kids need, at least initially. Along the way you will hear an amazing story of how a group of scientists in New York City and New Haven, Connecticut, in pursuit of a miraculous new kind of technology, stumbled upon an answer to a question that had plagued teachers for decades: Why do some perfectly smart kids have a hard time learning to read? You will see how a plethora of scientific knowledge about reading is now being used to create precise, focused reading instruction in classrooms and learn why, all too often, it is being ignored. The final section will lay out the skills that upper elementary school teachers and middle school teachers can build in their students in order to turn fledgling readers into great ones.

This chapter is an essential one. Just as you keep track of your child's vaccinations, parents should keep a sharp eye on the progress their children are making toward reading. Once your children have learned to decode, you need to make sure they're moving toward the mastery of reading. By the end of this chapter you'll be more sensitive to signs that your son or daughter is moving forward and you'll know the questions to ask if it looks like something might be going wrong.

WHEN READING FAILURE HITS HOME

Kelly Morelli, forty-nine, an accounting manager, and her husband, Michael, thirty-nine, a business agent for a local union near their home in central Vermont, have always been involved in the education of their two children. For years, the conventional wisdom among the Morellis' peers was that the local schools were A-OK. "We all felt like we had good choices," says Kelly. "Some schools in our valley are more creative and artsy, ours is more traditional, but on the whole, they are all considered to be good schools."

Kelly and Michael, though, are the kinds of parents who go the extra mile. When her older child, a boy named Morgan, started school, Kelly volunteered in the classroom just to keep her eye on what was happening. She was reassured. Morgan seemed to be doing fine. It was a different story with Kelly and Michael's daughter, Alanya. Even in kindergarten, it was clear that Alanya was doing great socially but didn't relish the academic part of the school experience the way her brother did. Different children are going to respond to school in different ways, Kelly reasoned. In the late spring of her first-grade year, with only two weeks before the start of summer vacation, Alanya's teacher told Kelly that Alanya was not reading at grade level.

Kelly had read enough articles in the newspaper about the roots of adult illiteracy to understand the gravity of what the teacher was telling her. Alanya needed help fast. Kelly knew that most research shows that if a child is not reading at grade level by third grade, the likelihood of them experiencing school failure grows exponentially. "You always hear about kids falling through the cracks but suddenly I realized this was happening to my daughter," says Kelly. "It was very upsetting."

Quickly, Kelly arranged a meeting with Alanya's teacher to figure out what could be done. Her first question was about timing. "I mean there were only a few weeks left in the school year. Why was I hearing about this now?" Alanya's teacher shrugged and handed Kelly a leaflet laying out her fee schedule. For $525, the teacher offered to provide Alanya with private tutoring sessions over the summer. Kelly was dismayed but her child was in a precarious spot. She knew she had to act.

Next, she arranged a meeting with the principal. First grade was drawing to a close but second grade loomed large. "I needed help figuring out the best and fastest interventions for my daughter," said Kelly. Instead, the principal seemed to have one foot out the door for her summer vacation. As Kelly tells it, the principal pointed out that the school year was almost over. Remedial instruction? She shrugged. "I would just encourage you to keep reading to her," she suggested. Furious, Kelly looked up the number of the school superintendent. Then she paused to assess the risk. She lives in a small town and she'd be creating an awkward dynamic with the principal, who would oversee her children's education for years to come, once she went above his head.

She did it anyway. The superintendent's response was far from satisfying. She told Kelly, "I'm a legal person. So if you want to come to me and tell me your principal or teacher is in violation of one of our guidelines or not in compliance with one of our rules, then I can help you." Beyond that, the superintendent was unwilling to intervene. Kelly felt like she'd been transported from her scenic

Vermont town into a short story by Kafka. It was true. The school wasn't breaking any rules. But her daughter hadn't learned to read. And the people in charge of her education didn't seem to have any idea how to fix this. A few days later, Kelly called a local private school, but she knew that the tuition there was beyond her means. Anguished, she thought, "Who is going to teach my seven-year-old how to read?"

THIS (ILLITERATE) AMERICAN LIFE

Imagine fifteen million variations on Alanya Morelli's story. Now you have a clear view of what is happening in American schools and the magnitude of the reading problem. In all kinds of neighborhoods, in all walks of life, our teachers are failing to instruct children in a way that provides a third of them with the skills they need to read.

Although it's a pervasive problem, it's not always easy to see. And that's because in many states, education officials have played a kind of shell game with the test scores. Watch closely and I'll show you how it's done.

There are two ways we measure how well our schools are teaching reading to our kids. The first is the so-called Nation's Report Card—a rigorous examination of how much children know taken from a representative sample of kids in a representative sample of schools from each state. The aim of that test is to keep policy makers informed about how much, as a nation, our kids are learning, and reading is one of the subjects that is assessed.

The second set of reading tests are administered to all children by each individual state. That test, which often goes by an acronym (for example, TAKS in Texas, MCAS in Massachusetts, and CSAP in Colorado), usually measures reading, math, and, in some states, other subjects as well. Results from those tests help provide oversight over our schools, help policy makers figure out where budget dollars need to be spent, and also ensure that states satisfy a federal law, No Child Left Behind, which requires all children in all states to be tested and found proficient in reading in fourth through eighth grade or face harsh sanctions. Now you might be rolling your eyes here and hissing, "Testing, testing, testing," and wondering why they just don't use the Nation's Report Card to measure state achievement. Good idea except for one problem—the Nation's Report Card or NAEP (for National Assessment of Educational Progress) tests assess only a small percentage of kids who reflect the population of that state. States need to test every kid.

To learn more about the strengths and weaknesses of standardized testing, you can go back to chapter 2, but for now, let's go back to the shell game. In the past, states had been allowed to come up with their own standards for the state tests, and in some places officials there made those standards laughably low. How low are those standards? The scores usually fall into categories: advanced, proficient, basic, and below basic. A federal report, which examined data from 2007, found that in thirty-one states, fourth graders that the state tests determined were at the low end of "proficient" would score not just "basic" but "below basic" when on the test for the Nation's Report Card. In other words, kids who got a low B on the state tests would get a D minus on the national one.

How would you know if your state is one of the ones that have dumbed down the test? Chance are, you wouldn't. Parents moving into a community look at the standardized test scores for the local schools before they buy their house. The state test scores—the ones that some state officials have been monkeying around with—are the only ones they see.

Not all states have opted to play this ugly game. If you live in

Massachusetts, Missouri, or South Carolina, you might want to send a fan letter to your state education chief. Your state standards are about on par with the ones on the Nation's Report Card. But if you live in, say, Tennessee, you should be getting mad right about now. And Georgia? In 2007, 88 percent of children in eighth grade there were declared proficient on the state reading test but only 26 percent were proficient on the national one. That means that while hardworking, taxpaying parents in Georgia were happily sending their kids off to schools that boasted high reading scores on state tests, only one in four of their eighth graders could read a chapter book or comprehend the *Wall Street Journal*.

To be fair, some of the worst offenders have since upped their standards. Realizing that lowering their standards is a shortsighted plan, about fourth-fifths of our states have decided to stop this charade altogether and signed on to teach and test what is called the Common Core State Standards in subjects that include reading and language arts. But it will take a while for those new standards to be adopted, even longer for those standards to be tested, and even longer to establish a timeline so parents can see if those test results reflect meaningful gains or declines. So for the time being, we're stuck gauging our kids' reading ability based in part on the old and, in some cases, bogus test results.

When your public officials dumbed down the tests, communities got hurt and so did kids. Sue Haynie, age fifty-eight, and her husband Kevin Daley, age fifty-six, real estate developers in Norwalk, Connecticut, watched with pride as young families moved in to the housing development they built, but their pride turned to puzzlement when those same families would move out again as soon as their kids reached school age. "They'd move a few towns away. And we couldn't figure out why. We believe in this community."

Eventually, Sue began scrutinizing the test scores in the local school. "The scores were a mixed picture but we were optimistic. We thought it would work out all right." But when Sue and Kevin's second son experienced reading failure, Sue took a closer look at those scores. "I was dismayed to find that about fifty percent of kids in Norwalk were reading at grade level, but because Connecticut has a less-than-stellar standard, an awful lot of kids were not being taught to read," she says. The communities down the road with top test scores were, by national standards, doing just okay.

Reading scores are worse for poor kids, for poor blacks and Hispanics, and for boys. But this is not just an underclass, or minority, or a boy problem. Kids in private school can struggle with reading also, but most private schools aren't compelled to publish the data or do anything more than "counsel out" the poor readers when they can't keep up. Federal statistics (and these are based on the Nation's Report Card, not those slippery state tests) tell us that about 20 percent of kids in parochial school and 19 percent of kids in private school—one in five—can attend a school that cost their parents $10,000, $15,000, even $25,000 a year and still end up functionally illiterate in fourth grade. Almost everywhere you look, at least 20 to 30 percent of kids struggle with reading.

But how can that be? You can walk in to almost any first- or second-grade classroom in the nation and see that learning to read is the order of the day. And indeed, there is almost always a core of children who are very excited about letters, words, sentences, and books. Research bears this out: about a third of kids, scientists tell us, learn to read almost spontaneously. No matter what kind of instruction they receive—good, bad, or none at all, that lucky third picks it up by what seems to be osmosis. When they are three, those children stare at meaningless black squiggles on a page. When they are five, those same black squiggles form themselves into words that convey real meaning. Then there is about a third of kids who need a few well-directed pedagogic shoves and they catch on to it. Without good instruction, that third may never be terrific readers, but they will muddle along. Finally there's the other third of students who require explicit instruction on how to break the reading code. If they don't get it, chances are good that they'll struggle with reading for a lifetime. Some may never learn to read competently at all. And the tragedy is, experts who work with kids who struggle say that if the right instruction is delivered in mainstream classrooms, somewhere between 95 and 98 percent of all children are able to learn to read.

What happens to kids like Alanya Morelli who don't get what they need from their school? Reading experts call them "instructional casualties." Most of them don't have neurological problems. They are not disabled. Their schools and, specifically, their primary school teachers have failed them.

In terms of outcomes, longitudinal research, the kind that follows kids for decades, tells a sad story. If your child is experiencing reading failure, it is almost as if he has contracted a chronic and debilitating disease. Kids who are not reading at grade level in first grade almost invariably remain poor fourth-grade readers. Seventy-four percent of struggling third-grade readers still struggle in ninth grade, which in turn makes it hard to graduate from high school. Those who do manage to press on—and who manage to graduate from high school—often find that their dreams of succeeding in higher education are frustratingly elusive. It won't surprise you to know that kids who struggle in reading grow up to be adults who struggle to hold on to steady work—they are more likely to experience periods of prolonged unemployment, require welfare services, and are more likely to end up in jail.

Even if your child is one of the lucky ones and is doing fine in reading, students who are poorly served by their primary schools end up being a drain on the public education system. Reading problems are the overwhelming reason why students are identified as having learning disabilities and assigned to special education, often an instructional ghetto of the worst kind.

It doesn't have to be this way. No area of education has been as thoroughly studied, dissected, and discussed as the best way to teach students to read. Seminal research and longitudinal studies from the National Academy of Sciences and the National Institute of Child Health and Human Development, combined with MRI (magnetic resonance imaging) and computerized brain modeling from the nation's top academic labs, provide a clear prescription for effective reading instruction. And yet that information is virtually unknown among teachers, parents, and those who serve on school boards. In nearly every conversation about reading instruction, educators talk about different pedagogical approaches and different philosophies, as if one is equal to another. And perhaps because some kids seem to learn to read like they learn to run, from observation and for the sheer love of it, it can appear like almost any kind of reading instruction can work with varying levels of success—on at least some kids. But researchers say they've come up with a straightforward formula that, if embedded into instruction, can ensure that 90 percent of children read. Scientists who conduct this research view the many different philosophies of reading that our primary schools espouse in the same way high-powered cancer specialists from Sloane-Kettering might view the oncology ward at a tiny community hospital. The doctors there have access to the new medicine that may cure your cancer but the specialists know that many hometown doctors are set in their ways and don't use it, only use some of it, or mix it in with some other not-so-effective treatments. And those specialists think it's a crying shame.

Intrigued? I know I was when all roads started pointing toward this research. But before we determine what good reading instruction looks like, let's take a step back and figure out why things are the way they are.

TEACHING READING IS ROCKET SCIENCE

In the nineteenth century, education was a humorless undertaking and reading instruction followed suit. Lessons on making meaning from words were imparted with a kind of grim rectitude. Students learned phonics, which is a method of systematically breaking down and sounding out words, by rote and repetition, and then were given religious and patriotic texts and encouraged to practice their reading. In 1839, statesman turned education expert Horace Mann, then secretary of the Massachusetts Board of Education, decided the time was ripe for expanding public education and making learning less of, well, a drag. According to his biographer, Jonathan Messerli, Mann visited Germany and then sought to import what seemed like the more naturalistic kind of reading instruction he witnessed there. In his book *Horace Mann: A Biography*, Messerli described what Mann was trying to transplant to the United States. "Instead of children being expected to learn individual letters by rote memory, then syllables, and finally words, they were given books with pictures of common objects. Underneath each picture was its simple name." Kids were taught to derive meaning from words by memorizing the look of the words, or looking at the picture and guessing, or reviewing the context and extrapolating, instead of sounding them out.

Mann's idea, later supported and expanded on by leading education figures like John Dewey and G. Stanley Hall, became known as a *whole-word* approach since the child learned to squeeze meaning out of a word, not by breaking it down but by looking at the word in its entirety. The enthusiasm for the whole-word approach lay, in part, in the fact that kids could get away from slicing and dicing words into sound chunks and instead focus on relating word to meaning, which, after all, is the point of reading.

To explain his views on education, Mann, who was later elected to Congress, used the same rhetorical techniques that would later be adopted by WWF (World Wrestling Federation) announcers and guests on *Meet the Press*. In other words, he napalmed the whole educational establishment. He charged that sounding out words was dull, authoritarian, harmful to students, bad for schools, and bad for the country. Mann complained about spelling, an extension of the phonics reading method, viscerally describing the "odor and fungousness of spelling book paper" from which "a soporific effluvium seem to emanate . . . steeping (the child's) faculties in lethargy."

The phonics supporters fired back. A full-throated debate about the best way to teach reading was most definitely *on*. For the next fifty or sixty years, the new way of teaching reading—the whole-word method—ruled. Whole-word instruction seemed fresh and contemporary, less top-down, rule-bound, and authoritarian than the old "drill it till you kill it" phonics. It's not a crazy idea. As we saw in chapter 1 on preschool, there is a strong connection between the spoken word and reading comprehension. It makes intuitive sense that the two processes should be similar. Children seem to spontaneously derive meaning from spoken language by learning to recognize certain words. As an infant, you learned the name of your annoying older sister when over and over, your annoying older sister walked into the room and your mom said her name, "Betsy." Your brain did not seem to be dismembering her name into the individual sounds, *Bet-SEE*. You derived meaning from the word *Betsy* by seeing Betsy and hearing your mom say "Betsy" at the same time, again and again.

Whole-word instruction called upon children to use the same natural and spontaneous method to learn to read as they did to learn their sisters' names. Students were repeatedly exposed to a small vocabulary of printed words until they built up a bank of words they could recognize—and then set about recognizing some more. When they encountered a word that stumped them, they were encouraged to examine the context in which they found the word and look for picture clues. Guessing was considered an important part of the learning process.

Whole-word instruction jived smoothly with some of the freshest and most innovative thinking about education at the time. In the 1940s, John Dewey was encouraging educators to see schools not as institutes for training, but as dynamic social institutions. Done right, the learning process was a way of shaping a new kind of citizen and preparing him for the responsibilities of participating in a democracy. "I believe that education is the fundamental method of social progress and reform," he wrote. Phonics, then, seemed like a leftover idea from another era, designed to squeeze the passion out of reading by imposing upon it a drab, lifeless, authoritarian set of rules.

By 1930, the last strictly phonics reader went out of print. And no one mourned the loss. *Dick and Jane* books, designed by the then eminent reading researcher William Gray, used those inscrutable characters Dick, Jane, Spot, and Puff to teach millions of Americans—many of them baby boomers—how to read. The material was simple. The picture carried the story and the words were allied to the picture. Notably, the teacher's major task during reading instruction was to introduce words slowly and with enough cues to their meaning so that their pupils would have contextual clues to help them figure out what the words meant, or take a good guess, until the sight of the word and its meaning became automatic. Basal readers, as textbooks based on this method of instruction are called, strictly limited the number of words they offered a child a chance to read. (The manufacturers boasted that for one set of textbooks, first-grade kids were exposed to 1,280 words. In third grade, they got the same 1,280 words with an additional 498 on top.) Many former students can recall that the limited vocabulary of basal readers made for mind-numbing prose. (See Spot Run! Run Spot Run!) The average third grader, who knows the meaning of about 44,000 words, could only find 1,778 of them represented on the page. The experts, though, were unequivocal: whole-word instruction was the way to go. Phonics, like the shoe hook or a clock key, seemed like an obsolete tool.

Then, predictably, the tide shifted again. In 1955, prevailing ideas about good reading instruction were given a brutal karate chop by a grumpy contrarian named Rudolf Flesch. In his book, *Why Johnny Can't Read*, Flesch launched a no-holds-barred attack on the whole-word method. His critique was powerful because it smacked of common sense. He demanded answers to a few simple questions: What happens to readers who learn to read from the context when they start reading books without pictures? And how can a reader be expected to recognize the millions of words in the English language? The back of *Why Johnny Can't Read* contained some quick lessons that parents could use to teach their kids to read using the old sound-it-out phonics method.

The whole-word supporters circled the wagons. Dewey had given teachers new lenses in their eyeglasses and encouraged them to see schools as institutions that would shape the society of tomorrow. From that perspective, Flesch's call for phonics was seen as an

Eisenhower-era quest to squash the messy, creative, passionate democracy of whole-word reading instruction. The kind of reading instruction a community promoted became a kind of litmus test—conservatives favored phonics and liberals, the whole-word method.

But in the decade after Flesch published his book, serious academics, many of them confirmed Lefties, started speaking out on behalf of phonics. The federal government, growing keenly aware of the social costs of reading failure, got into the act. In 1967, Harvard professor Jeanne Chall looked at different instructional models and followed kids' reading progress over time. Phonics, she found, was the best way to teach kids to read. In the years that followed, the whole-word approach began to evolve into something called "whole language." Recognizing and guessing might have its limitations, supporters argued, but so does sounding out words since English is, at times, an irregular language. Whole-language theory went something like this: just as children naturally and spontaneously derived meaning from speech by being exposed to the spoken word, children could naturally derive meaning from the written word by being exposed to plenty of newspapers, books, stories, and poetry. If teachers and parents were fervent readers and loved everything from *My Little Pony* to *Macbeth*, then they would transmit that passion for reading to their children. But how to tackle the achievement gap between middle-class and poor kids—which was then coming sharply into view? Reading specialists—taught that the whole-language method was the way to go and thrilled with a sense of social mission they had picked up at their colleges of education—tirelessly threw themselves at the problem, dedicating more time to reading, drama, writing, journaling: anything that would excite children who didn't have much exposure to books. And the large numbers of these kids—sometimes as many as a third in one class—who still struggled to learn to read? It was shrugs all around. In the privacy of the teachers' lounge, school administrators pinned that failure on parents who didn't know or couldn't afford to surround their children with the printed word at home.

Far away from the colleges of education and from classrooms, though, scientists began to reach a consensus around how children learn to read. And it was very different from what most teachers at the time would have predicted. Some of the most interesting break-throughs came from scientists who had only a passing interest in reading. They were too busy trying (and failing) to come up with a machine that would turn text into human speech. Their failure, though, changed everything.

THE READING MACHINE

In the 1950s, a well-known New York socialite and gentleman sci-entist named Caryl Haskins assembled a group of about ninety world-class scientists and put them to work in a laboratory above a necktie factory in midtown Manhattan. Haskins was a man for all seasons. He was extremely wealthy, looked great in a top hat and a tuxedo, and was a serious bug enthusiast. (He authored a book called *Of Ants and Men*.) And he was also something of a scientific Medici. He believed that the best scientific minds of his generation, if given the proper funding, could find a solution to the most vexing issues of the day. In the 1950s, at the behest of the federal govern-ment, he assembled a team of what would be known as Haskins scientists—young audio technology experts, psychologists, engineers, physicists, audiologists, and doctors—and charged them with devis-ing a reading machine to aid World War II veterans who had been blinded in battle. Haskins launched into the project with high hopes for a speedy and successful conclusion. Making meaning of speech, he figured, was basic, natural, and accomplished so often by so many. Perhaps it would take a few years, but making a reading machine seemed to Haskins like it would be an easy nut to crack.

The Haskins scientists got busy. They came up with an auditory Braille. The idea was that you could transcribe text into audio-Braille—for example, the letter *b* would be transcribed into dots that would cause the machine to make its own distinctive squeek or whistle—a kind of musical Morse Code. That worked just fine. But when they tried to feed in all the letters of a sentence and then a paragraph into the machine, the listener ended up reading at a laborious four words per minute instead of at a comfortable three hundred or so words per minute.

Over the next five years, Haskins scientists figured out how to make the machine "speak" faster, but the the reading rates were still too slow. Undeterred by that setback, the scientists began cooking up a device that would actually translate text into human speech. But no one involved in the project thought that would be easy. The production of human speech sound involves much more subtle processes than anyone had anticipated. The English language is composed of a predictable range of forty-eight or so sounds that are more or less represented by the twenty-six letters of the alphabet. But when, for example, you listen to your husband talk about his day over a glass of wine at dinner, what you are listening to is not strings and strings of isolated chunks of sound. Instead, you are hearing an almost infinite variety of sounds, each one affected by the sound that comes before it and the sound that comes after it. And to complicate matters even further, it turns out that you don't hear a single sound but three at once, an intertwined overlapping trio of sounds.

Over the years, Haskins scientists and scientists in other laboratories began looking at not just how we produce speech but how we understand it. Through a myriad of complicated experiments, they learned that human speech enters our ears and a little processor deep in our brains hears a full orchestral symphony of overlapping sounds. Then, in a period of time so small that we cannot be conscious of it, the processor deftly chops up the symphony into individual three-note chords, before separating each of those chords into the individual notes. In microseconds, the pattern of individual notes that remain is shipped to an eager librarian in our brain who takes a good look at it, then dives into our neurological file cabinet and roots around for the meaning of this pattern of now-disassembled sounds. If you've heard a nonsense word, like galk, the eager librarian will look and look but won't be able to find a match. If you've heard and understood the word before, she will analyze that set of sounds heard in that unique chord in that specific part of the symphony and assign it a meaning.

By this time, two decades had gone by. It was the groovy 1970s and Caryl Haskins had "retired" to become the head of The Carnegie Institute for Science in Washington, D.C. The Haskins Laboratories, now a renowned center for communications and speech production research, had moved to New Haven and become affiliated with Yale University and the University of Connecticut. Under the leadership of the charismatic Alvin Liberman, it raked in government and private grants. In one laboratory, a group of test babies might be clad in diapers and have giant headphones clamped on their heads. Down the hall, lisping school-age children might be getting examined by scientists coming up with new speaking strategies. Some of the scientists still pursued the laboratory's Holy Grail, to come up with a high-quality text-to-speech machine, and despite the formidable technical issues they had to overcome in order to devise a machine that could replicate the same complicated processes as a speaking human, came up with a working model in 1971.

All the research and thinking that was going on about speaking and hearing, and the connection between them provided a fertile medium for a breakthrough of a different sort—one that still reverberates in elementary schools around the nation. And it came about in an odd and indirect way. Alvin Liberman, the laboratory chief, was married to an intelligent, driven, and vivacious woman named Isabelle. She had obtained a Ph.D. in psychology from Yale back when university life wasn't very friendly to women. Then, she raised three children while working, first at a clinic for children with learning disabilities, and later, diagnosing and helping to treat those kids in a nearby hospital. Then, as now, most students she saw with learning disabilities were children who were struggling to learn to read.

The accepted theory of the day among educators was that people learned to read in the same way as it was commonly thought they learned to understand human speech. If a person encountered a word repeatedly in a book and figured out what it meant from the context, their brain naturally began to remember the appearance of the whole word and to assign meaning to it. Most educators and professors at teachers colleges didn't yet know that the Haskins scientists and others had already proven that understanding human speech was a lot more complicated than that.

The problem with dyslexics, according to the popular thinking among educators at the time, was that they couldn't perceive words correctly. Some believed dyslexics couldn't visually distinguish between letters, that some knot in their brain made dyslexics see letters backward or be unable to distinguish, say, an *m* from an *n*. Others believed dyslexics could not follow lines of text and that the words "ran off the page." There were all sorts of strange treatments for dyslexics back then aimed at improving their perception. Experts gave them worksheets of mazes so their eyes would learn to follow the lines. Other dyslexics were given tinted glasses to make black letters stand out against a white page more effectively. None of this, though, seemed to Isabelle Liberman to be helping the struggling readers she worked with learn to read particularly well.

In the late 1960s, Isabelle had begun working at Haskins. Unlike most reading specialists, she knew the literature and she knew the scientists doing this cutting-edge work on perceiving and producing the sounds of speech. She knew that understanding human speech depends on a complicated deconstruction of words into basic sounds. Her hunch was that the common thinking of the day was right, to a point. Reading was running on the same neurological highway as understanding human speech, requiring the same delicate choreography between the split-second sound dicer and the eager librarian. Except that if understanding speech is a neurological high dive, then reading was a triple back flip. What if in order for a child to understand a written word, his brain needed to translate that printed word into a (silent) chord of sound before feeding it into the making-sense-of-human-speech processor, which in turn passed it to the eager librarian? What if the problem with poor readers, Isabelle wondered, was not that they saw letters backward? What if the problem with poor readers was that they couldn't make the printed words on a page trigger the symphony of sound their brains needed to unravel in order to tease out its meaning?

"You have to realize how revolutionary it was," says Margie Gillis, now a senior scientist at Haskins, but then a twenty-one-year-old graduate student of Isabelle Liberman at the University of Connecticut. "Back then, we were treating dyslexics with mazes. We thought anyone who could distinguish the shapes of letters and words properly could learn to read." What reading specialists didn't realize is that in most cases, dyslexia wasn't about visual perception at all. Kids who couldn't read easily mistook "dad" for "bad" because their brains didn't reliably trigger a noticeably different sound from *b* and *d* and so the subtle visual differences had little significance. "We became convinced that this thing we called 'phonemic awareness'— the brain's ability to 'hear' the sounds represented by letters in a written word—might be a key skill most people needed to learn to read," says cognitive scientist Donald Shankweiler, who worked with Isabelle Liberman for years.

Throughout the 1970s and 1980s, Liberman and Shankweiler— and other scientists around the world who were working on the same issue—showed in different kinds of experiments that children who were likely to become poor readers were generally not as sensitive to the sounds of spoken words as children who were likely to become good readers. For example, a child destined to become a poor reader understands the word *bag*, but may not be able to clap for each of the three sounds in this word or to know that the last sound is what distinguishes *bag* from *bad*. A child who is destined to become a good reader could do it easily but the soon-to-be poor reader could not. The poor reader's processor for dissecting words into component sounds is less discerning. Which becomes a real problem when we ask those kids to execute the neurological triple back flip known as reading.

And here's a critical fact you need to know: scientists have shown again and again that the brain's ability to trigger the symphony of sound from text is not dependent on IQ or parental income. Some children learn that *b* makes the *buh* sound and that there are three sounds in *bag* so early and so effortlessly that by the time they enter school (and sometimes even preschool), learning to read is about as challenging as sneezing. When the feeling seizes them, they just have to do it. Other perfectly intelligent kids have a hard time locating the difference between *bag* and *bad* or a million other subtleties in language. Many studies have shown that phonemic awareness is a skill that can be strengthened in kids. And following that instruction in phonemic awareness, about one hundred hours of direct and systematic phonics instruction, that old Eisenhower-era bad boy, can usually get the job done and ensure that about 90 percent of kids have the fundamentals they need to become good readers.

But as you will see in the coming section, there are classrooms all over the country—in rich neighborhoods and poor neighborhoods—where kids aren't getting the instruction they need.

THE FIGHT

These scientific discoveries flew smack in the face of conventional wisdom about reading instruction. Educators shrugged it off as "too complicated." Others tried to make it political, dismissing this old/new way of looking at reading instruction as propaganda perpetrated by the conservatives trying to wrest control of schools. *Now wait a minute*, you're probably saying to yourself, primary school teachers wouldn't let politics get in the way of their training! They must know how to teach kids to read. They're teachers, right? An elementary school teacher who doesn't know how to teach reading would be like a plumber who doesn't know how to use a wrench! And what about all those highly paid directors of curriculum that school districts hire to ferret out the next best thing in teaching and learning?

I had exactly those thoughts. But the evidence would suggest that there was—and continues to be—a massive disconnect between laboratory and classroom. As these breakthroughs began to accumulate in the scientific literature in the fields of neurobiology, cognitive psychology, and linguistics, a huge swath of schools in this country were adopting reading programs based on the now-outmoded whole-language approach. In 1987, the entire state of California, and later the New York City Public School system, announced, with great fanfare, that they were switching to whole language. Primary school teachers were told to drop those musty old phonics lessons in favor of projects that helped kids become passionate about books. (Within ten years, reading scores in California had dropped abruptly and the program was abandoned. In 1995, New York City got a new schools' chancellor who dropped the whole-language approach in favor of phonics, and more recently, has adopted a mixture of approaches.)

On a classroom level, the majority of primary school teachers continue to be in the dark about how to teach reading. In a study conducted in 2006 and revised in 2007, Kate Walsh, a researcher at the National Council on Teacher Quality, a nonpartisan education reform group, examined seventy-two elementary education programs at selective and not-so-selective teachers colleges around the nation. She found that only 15 percent of schools of education were teaching aspiring teachers what the scientific community agreed were all the components of reading. In most schools she looked at, teacher educators portrayed reading instruction as a personal choice the novice teacher could make. Thus the method that has the support of thousands upon thousands of carefully designed, peer-reviewed scientific papers written by linguists, pediatricians, psychologists, neurobiologists, and engineers was mentioned as one approach among many. In nearly a third of the schools of education that Walsh looked at—many of which required students to take three, four, and sometimes five courses about reading—scientific reading instruction was never mentioned as a strategy to teach kids to read at all.

Well surely, you are thinking to yourself, new elementary-school teachers get instruction on how to teach reading somewhere, right? Actually, no. A few years ago, Connecticut education commissioner Mark McQuillan, frustrated with the reading scores in his state, added a new layer of certification for prospective teachers. In order to teach in Connecticut, teachers would have to take a test demonstrating that they understood how to teach reading in a way that jives with scientific findings. In the spring of 2010, the results of that new certification exam were announced. They were dismal, indeed. A third of the candidates who had successfully studied to become preschool and elementary school teachers in the state of Connecticut failed the test. The failure rate from one of the state's largest teacher preparation programs, the Connecticut State University system, which is underwritten with state dollars, exceeded 40 percent. If you live in Connecticut, and your elementary school child has a new teacher, there is a two in five chance that the teacher will not be able to provide your child with effective reading instruction. I'm not trying to pick on the Nutmeg State. Experts say that Connecticut is better at teacher education than some other states in the nation. Outside of Connecticut, your child could be learning to read from a teacher who has been taught even less.

In some places, school administrators report that there is a curious resistance to figuring out what the research on reading instruction says—and how to implement it. Anthony Pedriana has spent nearly thirty years in schools. For the first twenty, he'd been a classroom teacher; the last ten, an elementary school principal. In any given year in his classroom, and then in his school, about 30 percent of the children were reading below grade level. "We spent a lot of time scratching our heads and wondering why," says Pedriana. "The teachers I worked with were deeply caring and dedicated to seeing kids become fluent readers. But they didn't know how to teach them." In his book *Leaving Johnny Behind: Overcoming Barriers to Literacy and Reclaiming At-Risk Readers*, Pedriana writes about how a new teacher, skilled in the science of reading instruction, managed to get her entire class, save one, reading at grade level. Amazed, Principal Pedriana organized a teacher development day, which is when teachers learn new skills or brush up on old ones. He wanted all his teachers to learn the science of reading instruction that had made his new hire so successful. To his dismay, his loyal, dedicated staff almost mutinied. "I never encountered the kind of resentment displayed by some of the teachers that day," Pedriana says. "Those who behaved in this manner were probably decent individuals with good teaching records. They were merely expressing their derision for a program that bore little resemblance to how they had been trained. They were defending what they saw as their opportunity to be 'creative' in the classroom. Showing the efficacy of a science-based approach was not a message they were willing to accept under any circumstances. It was like asking a Christian fundamentalist to embrace the spirit of Allah."

Schools that know how to teach reading don't treat instructional practice like a personal preference. Last spring, in the third-floor library of the Solomon Juneau High School in the Bluemound Heights section of Milwaukee, members of the public, parents, community leaders, and pastors were invited to take a look at the new textbooks being considered for the kindergarten through eighth grade reading curriculum.

Even as state budgets are being slashed, Milwaukee schools are prepared to spend $6 million for new reading materials. They have to do something. Out of all the states in the union, African American fourth graders in Wisconsin, most of whom attend public schools in Milwaukee, have the lowest reading test scores in the country—9 percent are proficient. Test data released last spring showed that Wisconsin's African American eighth graders read less well than students in Wisconsin for whom English is a second language.

School administrators there decided to make sure all the schools used the same textbooks. That's a sound idea. Poor kids often move from school to school. If all schools were using the same textbook, theoretically, any teacher in any classroom will be providing the same kind of reading instruction. Asking community members to review the textbooks, though, gives the whole enterprise the feel of rearranging deck chairs on the *Titanic*. Teachers aren't going to be able to deliver good reading instruction unless they are briefed on research and shown explicitly how laboratory science can be translated into classroom practice. It would be a great service to brief community members on reading research, too. Explaining to teachers, parents, and community members the ways in which textbooks are supported (or not) by research is worthwhile. But getting community members to comment on textbooks—like they might express an opinion on what color the cafeteria should be painted or what tunes the marching band should play—seems like a disservice to everyone involved.

And here's a real tragedy. Desperate to stem reading failure, some schools in the district had adopted a program of scientifically based reading instruction a couple of years before and had seen their test scores for reading rise steadily. After getting input from the community last spring, the Milwaukee public schools adopted a new program and those enterprising schools learned that they would have to replace their textbooks' instructional methods and use ones that were more popular but less effective.

Reading failure is taking a toll on the kids and on the community.

Psychologist Steven Dykstra operates a mobile mental health unit in Milwaukee. Over time, he's become a reading activist. During the course of his day, he responds to calls from police officers, fire-fighters, school officials, even distraught parents with hard-to-manage teens. Any time a child is threatening to hurt himself or others, Dykstra is there. "Why do I care about reading instruction? I'll tell you why. I've seen children crying, children threatening to hurt themselves or hurt others. I've talked to kids who are up on the roof." These children obviously have many problems, but at the heart is often their struggle at school and at the center of that struggle is that they can't read. "They feel shame. They feel stupid. They know their life will never get better unless they learn to read." Dykstra begins counseling them, and frequently visits them at home and in their school. "Often their parents are assuming the school will teach those children how to read. But when I go to the school, I talk to teachers who simply don't know how to do it. Their student, my patient, is seriously contemplating suicide because they don't know how to read—and no one is helping these children."

WHAT YOUR CHILD NEEDS TO SUCCEED

Without turning this chapter into a primer on phonics, let me give you a SparkNotes version of explicit phonics. What you are looking for is this: in kindergarten, your child should be learning consonant sounds and short vowel sounds in isolation. The letter *b* makes the sound *buh* and *ah-eh-ih-ah-uh*. By first grade, *ah-eh-ih-ah-uh* should be topped with *aye-ee-i-oh-you*. First graders should be learning to blend sounds into words and be "sounding out" words in sentences. They should also be learning the forty-four sounds in the English language and the seventy-seven common ways to spell them (th, sh, ch, wh, ck, ay, ai, eight). Then come the rules that govern short and long vowel sounds. (When a word ends in *e*, the vowel says its own name.) To get a more detailed picture of explicit phonics instruction you can go to www.nrrf.org, which is a Web site maintained by the National Right to Read Foundation.

Many districts have adopted what they call a "balanced literacy" approach to reading. If school administrators describe their reading program that way, you'll need to ask a few more questions. In some schools, balanced literacy means that pre-K teachers work on letters and letter sounds. Kindergarten, first-, and second-grade teachers deliver an orderly progression of explicit phonics lessons and, as the children become competent and confident readers, push them to discover the best that literature and nonfiction have to offer while doggedly building up their comprehension through weekly word study, spelling tests, and story analysis. Balanced literacy can also mean something very different—and something that looks a lot like a whole-language approach. Some teachers provide a portion of the kids with a smattering of phonics (most schools now concede that some kids do need phonics to help figure out the code) and also encourage them to guess words from illustrations, and later, from context. As the children (hopefully) get more competent at reading, those teachers minimize the study of language and devote their time and energy to getting them excited about words, reading, and books. If you care about your child's school success, you'll want more of the former kind of instruction and less of the latter.

Once you've seen science-based reading instruction delivered well, you'll want it for your kids. For six years, Kristina Matuskiewicz, a kindergarten teacher at Edna C. Stevens Elementary School in Cromwell, Connecticut, believed that, like all the teachers at her tidy suburban school, she was helping to make good readers. She read them stories, she identified words and described their meaning, she offered them a variety of good books and worked to shift them to independent reading. "Each teacher had their own approach to teaching reading," says Matuskiewicz. The problem was, none of their approaches were working very well. In 2007, only 70 percent of the third graders were proficient in reading. Not only that, each year, some 33 children out of 489 kids in the pre-K–second grade school required outside support in reading—a program that was costly for the school and for the district. The principal, Lucille DiTunno, decided the school needed to take another approach. First, she asked her teachers to establish a "literacy block"—ninety minutes a day dedicated to reading. Three years ago, DiTunno paid $28,000 to Literacy How, then a division of Haskins Laboratories, to bring consultants to Edna C. Stevens Elementary School every week for a full year to teach teachers about the scientifically proven methods that help kids learn to read. The first meeting, says Literacy How consultant Wendy North, was a disaster. "We got off on the wrong foot," says North. The teachers felt like they were being blamed for the struggles of kids they hadn't taught in years. Instead of directing the anger at the inadequate instruction they had been given at teachers college, she says, they felt humiliated and angry that outside experts were being brought in to teach what they already knew—how to teach reading.

North persevered. These days, kindergartners in Matuskiewicz's class get a different kind of instruction than their older brothers and sisters ever did. During the first week of kindergarten, Matuskiewicz sits with each child and determines if he or she knows the letters and their corresponding letter sounds. The skill levels of the children are variable. So, class work in the autumn has to do with "sorting"—identifying letters and connecting them to sounds. At one of the small tables, Samantha, a bright, round-faced little girl with luxuriant flaxen curls, sits with her glue stick in the air, trying to figure out whether a picture of a nail belongs with words that start with *n* or *g*. For her, at this moment in time, the letter-sound correspondence is far from automatic. "Nail, nail, *n*-ail," Samantha whispers to herself. Matuskiewicz starts teaching letter sounds with *n*, *m*, *f*, and *s* for a reason. Since those sounds are easiest to sustain with the mouth, they supply kids with more of an opportunity to catch hold of the individual sound. Back at knee level, Samantha glues the picture of a nail under the letter *g*, then lifts it off the paper and presses it down with great finality under the letter *n*. Later, Matuskiewicz describes how she interprets the child's process. The confusion between *n* and *g*? "It doesn't mean she's not smart," says Matuskiewicz. "It just means she needs some practice."

Some of the kids with a keen sense of phonemic awareness are already moving on to what is called in teacher-speak "decodable text"—little books with single lines of text made up of words that can be sounded out with ease. Books like *Sal Has a Pal* and *Dad and Ted* are unlikely to be winning a Newbery Medal any time soon, but they help reinforce the basic strategies. After about thirty minutes, all the children stop their work and, using a broad hand motion for each sound, sing what is known as "the vowel song" with great gusto. When the chorus of cheerful voices begins to die away, North and Matuskiewicz look pleased. "The rap against phonics is that there is too much drilling," says North. "But look at this classroom. No one is suffering here."

First-grade teacher Angela DiStefano, a twelve-year teaching veteran, says the Literacy How approach to reading has changed her professional life forever. "Before that, I thought it was my job to teach kids to share my enthusiasm for reading." Now, she teaches them to read with explicit instruction on how to sound out words. Not long ago, she gave a seminar for first-grade parents to teach them some rules about vowels (for example: vowels make their short sound in closed pattern words like *tap* and the long sound in open pattern words like *hi*, *so*, and *my*) so parents could reinforce the lessons at home.

The Literacy How approach has increased the scores on interim tests, and results from the first third graders who learned to read this way are expected to be high. Already, only three children per year are now being referred for the costly reading support, a massive savings for the district. DiStefano says that the new program has made her relationship with parents more straightforward. "Before, we might say, 'That child isn't reading!' And we'd shrug. We didn't know what to do. Now we can sit with a parent and say, 'Your child is struggling to understand the rule that when a word ends with *e*, the middle vowel says its own name.' And we can describe our plan to reteach that and get parents to emphasize that at home and get that child back on the path to reading success."

THE MYTH OF CATCHING UP

When you become a parent, you wake up in a new universe. And for few years, it can be a mighty scary one. Things that in the past seemed perfectly innocent now present a clear and present danger. Marbles? Choking hazard! Toys made in China? Lead poisoning! Conventionally grown strawberries? Sweet-smelling pesticide bombs! By the time your child heads to school, most of the hypervigilance is, blessedly, a thing of the past. Maybe Number Two has come along. Or maybe you've gotten your sea legs as a parent and gained some assurance that the little things you do wrong or right are just that—little things. I don't want to send you back to the old days, when a multicolored marble looked as dangerous as a machete, but you need to know this: if your child is not progressing in reading, you need to act and act now.

When children enter kindergarten—even in private schools

where each class is hand-selected—they come as they are. Some have been in preschool classrooms for a year or two. Others have never actually spent time as one of a group. Some seem sophisticated enough for a cameo on *Gossip Girl*. Some seem as vulnerable as lambs. Their academic skills are variable, too. Some are already reading chapter books, some know the sounds that the letters make, others are only dimly aware that the red octagonal at the end of their street means "stop."

But from the time they are in kindergarten through third grade, all children need to be making weekly progress toward mastering what we now know is the complicated process of squeezing meaning from text. In the early years, children should be learning a list of "recognize words"—high-frequency words like *at, and, the, then, what,* and *when*. By the end of kindergarten and into first grade your child's teacher should be providing explicit phonics lessons—consonants, consonant blends, short vowels, long vowels that are followed and controlled by the silent but powerful *e*. If your child is being taught "recognize words" but not decoding, you need to ask a few more questions. By second grade, kids should not be trying to recognize new words or to figure out words by picture clues. They should be breaking words down into sound chunks and getting quicker and more sophisticated as the weeks go by.

Check in with your child's teacher frequently to make sure she is moving forward. You don't want to hear vague assurances such as "your child is doing well" or "your child is poorly behaved," that she raises her hand before speaking (or not), or knows how to use glue. Your child's teacher should be able to describe to you in some detail your child's incremental movement forward or the specific area where she is falling short.

Kindergartner Jack Tillotson, who lives in a rural area about an hour and a half from Minneapolis, Minnesota, didn't seem to be grasping the connection between letters and their sounds. His kindergarten teacher met with his mother, Tammy Tillotson, herself a teacher trainer, and suggested that she read to her son more often. Although the teacher was young, Tammy saw that she had some old-school views on reading: she thought that if Jack was exposed to more literature, he would eventually figure out some of the fundamentals he was lacking. To Tammy, who has an advanced degree in education, that didn't compute. Tammy has two older sons who do very well in school and love to read. The Tillotsons' house is filled with all kinds of reading material: science books, sports books, fantasy stories, video gaming and wildlife magazines. "Exposure," says Tammy, wryly, "is not the problem."

By first grade, Jack was falling farther behind. Out of a perverse sense of kindness, Jack's teachers began scaling down their expectations for him. When other children were asked to read a page, Jack was asked to read half a page. When they were given ten spelling words, Jack was given five. Beyond having him do less, Tammy recalls, "the teachers had no good ideas how to help him move forward." Tammy asked to have their son evaluated. Her suspicions were confirmed. Jack wasn't reading anywhere near grade level. Tammy met with a team of specialists in her school to discuss what could be done. "These are people I've worked with before. People I knew. I didn't expect any special treatment but I did expect a certain level of respect." She was in for a shock.

In the meeting, the special education teacher flatly refused to provide Jack with extra instruction or even help Jack's teacher figure out what instruction would help Jack's progress. "She said that Jack was not far enough behind. She suggested that we wait until third grade, when the gap between Jack and the rest of his peers had grown larger, and then he would be far enough behind to qualify for special services." Tammy is still emotional when she recalls the meeting. "I was, like, are you serious?" her voice rising an octave. This advice, Tammy knew, contradicts nearly every bit of research on reading difficulties. As a rule, early intervention around reading problems works best. Tammy figured the learning team had to know this. But here they were, the school staff, people she knew, colleagues, condemning her child to a long, hard road that would most likely lead to school failure. "It was then I realized that it was up to us to become knowledgeable about what Jack needed and figure out how to get his teachers to supply it."

When your first-grade child isn't making progress in reading or seems to have reached a plateau, you need to move quickly. Ask for a meeting with his or her teacher, and if that's not effective, ask for a meeting with the reading specialist at the school. Your first question for the reading specialist should be asked privately. Ask her to describe his or her training to teach reading. It seems like a tactless question, like asking your dentist if he knows his way around teeth. In some schools, the job of reading specialist is given to a teacher with a high level of training in teaching kids to read. Sometimes she is a teacher who year after year was able to get and keep all her students at grade level. Often, though, the job of reading specialist is given to a longtime teacher as a reward. If you are meeting with a reading specialist who is the latter rather than the former, downscale your expectations for the meeting. Once the teacher and specialist and maybe the principal have assembled, you're looking for a plan of action. You don't want to hear anyone say, "She's just not ready," or "He'll catch up," or "We need to wait another year until he is farther behind in order to get help." If you hear "Maybe we need to hold him back until he is ready to read," you'll need to ask even more questions. There are some reasons for holding kids back that may make sense (although the research here is not clear). But for most struggling readers, learning to read is not a question of maturity. The real question is: "What about next year's instruction will be different from this year's instruction?" Giving your child the same ineffectual method of reading instruction for another year is not going to help. You want to leave that meeting with a thoughtful, targeted plan of attack, one that starts tomorrow. If you don't get it, you may need to find the resources to bring in a specially trained tutor.

For her part, Tammy Tillotson did the educational equivalent of lifting a car that had rolled over her child. She signed up for a forty-hour training on how to teach struggling readers—one that emphasized a direct, explicit, and multisensory approach to phonemic awareness and, later, phonics. She began volunteering in the classroom—providing top-drawer reading instruction—and supplying Jack's teachers with supplemental materials. Jack's still not a stellar reader, but he's gotten better. In the classroom, she has to be subtle about the kind of help she is offering. She's gotten a strong sense that she's treading on thin ice and she is, after all, only a volunteer. Outside of school, the value of what she is offering is getting wider recognition. It turns out there are many kids in the area who need what Tammy can now supply. Not long ago, she was hired by a local philanthropic organization to provide supplemental reading instruction at a local community center. Her classes are packed.

TURNING READERS INTO REALLY GOOD READERS

Once your child has figured out how to decode words and can actually read in a sustained way, then a chunk of his schooling should be focused on helping him squeeze meaning and richness out of the experience. You remember the whole-language ideas about exposing kids to print through fiction, poetry, newspapers, and drama? It is the wrong way to teach kids to read. But getting kids excited about the written word is a *great* way to turn fledgling readers to voracious readers.

And here's where all parents should step up to the plate. You've been reading to your child, great. Don't stop. Books on tape in the car work, too. But now that she is a reader, surround her with print. Get a newspaper delivered. Get her a library card and make the library a regular stop, like the grocery store and the dry cleaner. And get over your view of what "proper" book reading looks like—fiction, nonfiction, comic books, how-tos, mysteries, sports biographies, magazines about current events, fast cars, sleek airplanes, or video gaming. Open the door wide. Find ways to bring what she is reading into the conversation. Ask questions like: What kind of book is it? What is the setting? What happens? What do you like/not like about the way the author writes? Similar but more formal versions of this should be happening at school, but parents can reinforce this at home. Watch for it.

If your child is reading and sampling a wide enough variety of material, he will be encountering a lot of words in print that he doesn't know. He should be able to sound out the word. How he learns to derive meaning from unfamiliar words will determine whether he grows. First, encourage him to figure out the meaning of unfamiliar words from their context, for example, what could *propulsion* mean based on the words that came before it and after it? Then, see if he can tease out the meaning of the word by finding its root. For instance, the word *propel* is hidden in *propulsion* and gives a strong suggestion for the meaning of the word.

Teachers help comprehension grow through the systemic study of words. Yes, weekly vocabulary words. Kids who study words—by this I mean systematically learning their meanings—have larger vocabularies but are also better readers. It's not too effective for the teacher to hand out a list of ten words and have kids look them up and then take a test. They need to hear the words, see them, speak them, and write them that week and in the weeks that follow.

Word lists alone, though, aren't enough. Kids encounter an average of three thousand new words a year—more than eight a day. Unless the entire school day is going to be given over to word study (and pretty much no one thinks this is a good idea), teachers must instruct children on how to shave off chunks of an unfamiliar word and tease out its meaning by studying suffixes, prefixes, and where certain common word roots come from and their meaning.

Comprehension, fluency, and stamina should be growing stronger as your child moves through school. Schools need to ensure that happens. So do parents. Do your part.

THE TAKE AWAYS

1. Learning to read and to read very well are crucial to your child's well-being.

2. Find a school that uses scientifically based reading instruction. Find out what that is, and make sure your child's school is doing it.

3. Make it clear to your child's teacher that you expect frequent, detailed reports on your child's progress in obtaining the basic skills in reading.

4. If your child is not moving forward steadily, be prepared to take action. "Wait and see?" Nope. Watchful waiting is a good practice for many aspects of child rearing. Progress in early reading is *not* one of them.

5. Be prepared to encounter some confusion and defensiveness from the people you'd think are the experts. Do not be deterred.

6. Throughout elementary school and middle school, teachers should be engaging in increasingly sophisticated forms of word study.

7. After second grade, surround your child with all kinds of books and make what she's reading a big topic of dinnertime conversation. Listen to the way she talks about books to ensure that her comprehension continues to deepen.

CHAPTER FIVE

WHEN MATHEMATICIANS GET ANGRY

*If you ask your mother for one fried egg for breakfast
and she gives you two fried eggs and you eat both of
them, who is better in arithmetic, you or your mother?*
—FROM "ARITHMETIC" BY CARL SANDBURG
(1878–1967)

WHEN M. J. MCDERMOTT got in front of the microphone to address the Seattle Public School Board a couple of years ago, she didn't realize that she was about to become a folk hero among some of the most highly educated parents around the country. She was president of the parents' association at the local public elementary school where her two children attended fourth grade, and the word around the hallways was that the middle school math program wasn't up to snuff. McDermott, the mother of twins, holds an advanced degree in atmospheric science and is a weather forecaster at a local TV station. She is able to do her job well because she is able to use math accurately, confidently, and efficiently. She wanted her children to be able to do the same. As the saying goes, if you want something done, ask a busy mom. McDermott made time to reach out to principals and collect the math curriculums and textbooks being used in other elementary schools and middle schools in her district. McDermott, who has a wide smile and stylish blunt-cut hair, says math "has always been very important to me." When she took a look at what she had collected, she found curriculums and textbooks that seemed too broad, too jumbled, and tried to tackle too many topics in one year. McDermott was worried. From her experience as a successful math student, she knew the primary years are key. By eighth grade, or maybe ninth, children should be prepared to take algebra, the start of a sequence of high school math that in turn sets the cornerstone for college-level coursework. To McDermott's eye, children who studied math in the Seattle public schools weren't getting out of the starting gate. "The curriculum the school district laid out wouldn't give them the skills they need to get to college-level mathematics," she said. This was, she said, "math for English majors."

So, standing in front of a scratchy microphone and holding the textbooks the district used, she explained to the subcommittee on math curriculum—and later on in a video posted on YouTube— why Seattle needed to rethink their math instruction. Page by page, she leafed through the written curriculum and textbooks, pointing out problems. Forty-five pages of the textbook devoted to using a calculator? Too much! Using illustrations of pizza to explain the concept of fractions to middle schoolers? "That's just infantile," said McDermott. One assignment in a middle school textbook particularly got on McDermott's liberal nerves. It featured a photograph of a smiling African American girl and encouraged children to identify their favorite number and keep a journal about that number. "What is the implication there?" she snorted. "That African American girls can only journal about numbers instead of doing real math? Twelve-year-olds should be working on pre-algebra!" She demanded a pared-down, well-sequenced, rigorous math program for her kids.

The school district leaders listened—and yet opted to do nothing. But McDermott's presentation caught the attention of other parents from around the state. Eleven miles away in a Seattle suburb, Lyng Wong, forty-five, and her husband, John Chu, forty-three, found that McDermott had articulated some of their concerns about the kind of math their son was learning. In kindergarten, their son's teacher taught the children to use a calculator instead of emphasizing adding and subtracting. In the early grades, Wong noted, his homework seemed too easy and the topics jumped around without an obvious progression. Concerned, Wong and Chu began to supply him with worksheets so he could practice his math facts and problem-solving. But when his teacher got wind of it, she reprimanded them. "She told us not to go ahead of the class. That he might learn math wrong," recalls Wong. Wong and Chu leafed through their son's math textbook and saw a kind of emotionalism in math they found unfamiliar and a little bizarre. For example, numbers divisible by 2 and 5 were described as "friendly" and numbers divisible by seven as "unfriendly."

Wong and Chu asked for a meeting with the principal. "The principal told us the point of math instruction was to teach children to approach a math problem in a generic sense and to learn life skills involving math." Worthy goals, conceded Wong and Chu, but the math instruction wasn't becoming deeper and more complex. The couple were relying on primary school math instruction to supply the foundation skills so their son could tackle pre-algebra in the middle school years. The principal tried to soothe them. She told us not to worry, recalls Lyng. "She said, 'Not everyone will be an engineer or scientist.'"

Wong, who was educated in public schools in Los Angeles, and Chu, who was educated in Brazil, both hold advanced degrees in engineering. Chu, who helped invent the two-dimensional bar code, runs a division of a well-known tech company. During their meeting with their son's principal, both Wong and Chu struggled to contain their frustration.

McDermott, Wong, and Chu began meeting up with other math-minded parents—many of them math professors, engineers, science professors, and computer scientists—to push schools around the state to overhaul their math program. Within two years, the nonpartisan group they joined, Where's the Math? was attracting hundreds of parents to their public meetings—and pressuring state legislators to improve math standards in the state.

The Great Math Battle of Washington State is hardly an isolated conflict. In the last five years, similar skirmishes around math instruction have broken out around the country. Highly educated parents in California, in suburban New Jersey, and on the Upper East Side of Manhattan, many of whom hold advanced degrees and work in science, in technology, or in financial services, or as entrepreneurs, are leading the charge. Some districts have resisted their efforts. Faced with a push to improve math instruction in Penfield, New York, the superintendent there told a *New York Times* reporter that the trouble stemmed from "helicopter parents" who, confronted with a different kind of math instruction, "didn't know how to support their children at home." These activist parents have been dubbed the Nerd Herd. They've been dismissed as "those math fanatics." But they're already having a far-reaching impact. Their critical perspective and pointed questions have prompted a wave of affluent school districts around the nation to rethink the way they teach math.

What exactly makes a good math program? Should we look for the kind of traditional math instruction in our children's school that emphasizes skills and drills? Or throw our support behind an "inquiry and exploration" model? And if we want a balance, what is the right balance? The answers are far from clear. But in laboratories all over the world, research teams are coming up with tantalizing new evidence that many believe will turn our old ideas about math instruction on their heads. Around the country, forward-looking educators are thinking about ways to integrate the tsunami of scientific research on math cognition into the math classrooms of tomorrow.

In this chapter, you'll find out why, for better or worse, schools teach math the way they do. We'll travel to an animal laboratory at Duke University in North Carolina where you'll see monkeys estimating, adding, and exhibiting an astounding sensitivity to numbers. And you'll hear why some cutting-edge scientists believe these monkeys may hold the key for improving the math ability in American students. You'll also be introduced to a new kind of math curriculum that is teaching children math in a way that echoes and enhances our innate math skills. At the end of this chapter you'll learn the things you can do right now to help your child get and stay on the right path.

Overall, schools in the United States are doing a very poor job instructing our children in math. In our country, a shocking number of children grow into adults with the math abilities that verge on the math version of dyslexia, called dyscalculia. And there are those who do okay in math in school but can't do much math later in life. According to a 2008 report issued by the U.S. Department of Education, 78 percent of adults in this country cannot explain how to compute the interest paid on a loan, 71 percent cannot calculate miles per gallon on a trip, and 58 percent cannot calculate a 10 percent tip for a lunch bill.

The trouble starts early. According to the 2007 Nation's Report

Card, 27 percent of eighth graders could not correctly shade one-third of a rectangle and 45 percent could not solve a word problem that required dividing fractions. International comparisons paint an unsettling picture. Results from the 2007 Program for International Student Assessment (PISA) showed that fifteen-year-olds from the United States ranked seventeenth among industrialized nations, above Greece, Israel, Turkey, Chile, and Mexico but below Korea, Finland, Switzerland, Japan, Canada, the Netherlands, New Zealand, Belgium, Australia, Germany, Estonia, Iceland, Denmark, Slovenia, Norway, France, and the Slovak Republic, and well below cities like Shanghai and Singapore.

American parents are beginning to understand that our children must learn math early and well in order to thrive. In a study published in *Science* in 2008, researchers found that solid primary school instruction had a larger effect on long-term mathematical achievement than the child's father's education, their socioeconomic status, or the parents' income. Math knowledge builds on math knowledge. Without a firm foundation, high school math is too difficult to tackle. College freshmen who haven't taken these upper-level math courses will find themselves shut out of a science, social science, computer, technology, or engineering major. In addition, a strong foundation in mathematics seems to provide children with a certain level of academic resilience. Kids who complete Algebra II are twice as likely to graduate from college as students who don't take it. And more than ever, once they enter the workforce, math is a skill they'll need to have and use.

Researchers at the American Diploma Project, who are advising governors on how to raise state standards, estimate that in the next ten years, 62 percent of entry-level workers in America will need to be proficient in algebra, geometry, data interpretation, probability, and statistics.

Many parents have their eyes on an even bigger prize. When it comes to the science and engineering sectors of our economy, the world is already flat. It starts in college. Undergraduate classes are being filled with very bright foreign-born students who have acquired a solid foundation in math in their home countries. Armed with those skills, foreign-born students educated abroad are partaking of the American dream in a way that many American-educated students cannot. According to the National Science Foundation, 40 percent of doctoral holders in so-called STEM (science, technology, engineering, and mathematics) professions here are foreign born. Technology start-ups, a volatile field where fortunes are made, lost, and made again, are now attracting scientists who got their early years of education elsewhere. An estimated one-fourth of all new U.S. engineering and technology businesses established between 1995 and 2005, including Google and eBay, and half of all business

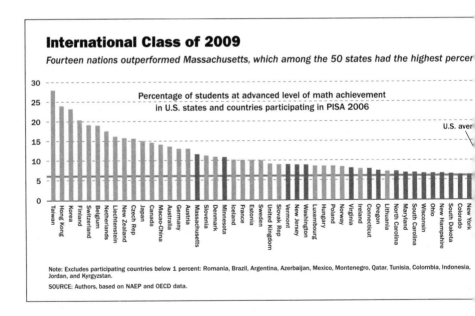

International Class of 2009

Fourteen nations outperformed Massachusetts, which among the 50 states had the highest percer

Percentage of students at advanced level of math achievement in U.S. states and countries participating in PISA 2006

Note: Excludes participating countries below 1 percent: Romania, Brazil, Argentina, Azerbaijan, Mexico, Montenegro, Qatar, Tunisia, Colombia, Indonesia, Jordan, and Kyrgyzstan.

SOURCE: Authors, based on NAEP and OECD data.

start-ups in high-tech Silicon Valley had a foreign-born scientist or engineer as a key part of the team.

Unfortunately, in most states in our country, it seems, our schools are setting the threshold for acceptable levels of math skills too low to produce a generation of kids who will be able to compete in our global economy. According to the 2007 Trends in International Mathematics and Science Study, only 7 percent of U.S. fourth graders scored at the advanced level on the international test, whereas in Singapore, 38 percent of fourth graders were advanced. How serious is the problem with math achievement in American? Stanford economist Eric Hanushek and his colleagues crunched the numbers from the Nation's Report Card test and from the PISA and compared foreign countries to each state in the union in order to see how our kids are stacking up in the global sweepstakes. Here's how it looks:

dents achieving at the advanced level in math.

If your child is being educated in Massachusetts, you probably feel okay. You can see that your child stands a chance in this New World. But if your child is being educated in West Virginia, New Mexico, or Mississippi, she is being inadequately prepared for the jobs of tomorrow.

. . . AND CARRY THE TWO

For a subject that is known for having One Right Answer, math, and how to teach it, has been the subject of a long and contentious debate. While it's not as old as the Reading Wars, it's close. Until the 1920s, math instruction worked like this: You learned how to execute problems. Then you executed them. Simple. Straightforward. And dry as dust. In 1923, the National Committee on Mathematical Requirements issued a report chiding teachers for boring their students nearly to death: "The excessive emphasis now commonly placed on manipulations is one of the many obstacles to intelligence progress. On the side of algebra, the ability to understand its language and to use it intelligently, the ability to analyze a problem, to formulate it mathematically, and to interpret the result must be dominant aims. Drill in algebraic manipulations should be limited to those processes. . . . It may be conceived throughout as a means to an end, not an end it itself."

By the 1950s, though, not much had changed. In early elementary school, math was an afterthought. Schools of education taught teachers math education through the lens supplied by influential Swiss psychologist Jean Piaget. In Piaget's view of human development, a baby's mind was tabula rasa: he believed that no "a priori or innate cognitive structures exist in man." Discussing mathematical concepts with a child was like talking to a parrot: you might succeed in cueing up some rote response, but the parrot was not learning. A child, according to Piaget, could only really grasp the concept of numbers at around six or seven. They could grasp the idea of mass at age eight and weight at age ten. Before that, children were simply too concrete in their thinking to comprehend much more.

In most places in the country, math instruction didn't start until first or second grade and only got going in earnest in third or fourth grade. When it did, math instruction revolved around the rote memorizing of math facts like 2 plus 2 is 4 and the multiplication table. There were hard-and-fast rules for solving multi-digit multiplication and long division problems and manipulating fractions and decimals. Students were instructed to work through problems in the prescribed way—they were graded for speed and, of course, accuracy. Plenty of people learned math this way—but plenty didn't.

In 1957, when the Russians launched *Sputnik*, there was a fresh round of public soul searching about why so few Americans excelled at math and what schools could do about it. Faced with a cold war defeat, many distinguished mathematicians, scientists, and education professors at prominent universities around the United States and Europe began collaborating on overhauling the K–12 math curriculum. The aim was to create a new generation of technological whiz kids by teaching them math in a new way aimed at sparking their creativity and promoting innovation. In the early 1960s, that math reform group unveiled their new framework. Although there were several variations of the so-called New Math, nearly all of them asked teachers to approach the subject with more inquiry and research and less reliance on rote memorization, recommendations that have lasted to this day. In addition, some strains of New Math also introduced college-level concepts like set theory, vector spaces, and matrices in middle and high school. Teachers, many of whom were not trained in higher-level concepts, found it hard to teach New Math. Kids found it incomprehensible. In 1972, 3.6 million ninth graders took math. In 1976, the number was 294,000. After a brief tango with New Math, most districts returned to the kind of math our grandparents would recognize—fixed, abstract, and based on skills and drills.

This industrialized approach to teaching math still didn't work that well. Lots of students could execute the algorithms but hated math. They knew how to multiply, but they didn't see how to connect math to their everyday lives. The late 1970s and early 1980s saw a loosening of many cultural norms—and math instruction seemed ripe for an update. In 1989, the most powerful group of math educators and teachers of math educators—the National Council of Teachers of Mathematics—announced that math education would once again be overhauled. In the 1990s, the NCTM deemed, math teachers would put a premium on what their guidelines called "problem setting and solving, on conjecture and hypothesis, on exploration and inquiry. Students were to debate and discuss ideas, become mathematical authorities alongside teachers and textbooks, and justify their answers with reason and logic instead of mastery of rote process." Math education should emphasize critical thinking, underlying concepts, and the connectedness of those concepts to everyday life. The 1989 guidelines aimed to democratize the subject—math was for everyone and everyone should be able to learn math.

The guidelines were an attempt to get educators to think about math instruction in a fresh, highly sophisticated way. What the NCTM didn't bargain on was that in many schools, levels of math knowledge among teachers were very low. And those math-wary educators saw the new guidelines as confirmation that they could and should teach mathematics-lite. Because of the prevailing ideas about how children developed their math thinking, in preschool and kindergarten math instruction consisted of counting and quantity—identifying which pile of M&M's is bigger and which is smaller. In primary school, children were taught what numbers represented and how to think about addition, subtraction, multiplication, and division in different ways. Calculators were used to solve equations: anyone could add, subtract, multiply, and divide. "Coming up with your own unique way of solving the problem"—even using highly inefficient strategies—was championed. In many places, original thinking was more important than getting the right answer. Math was taught using colorfully illustrated textbooks and emotive language.

Conservatives fired back—and the back-to-basics faction of mathematicians joined in, too. Ten years later, the NCTM issued another set of guidelines—more conciliatory in tone—in an attempt to mollify their critics. This time NCTM made an eloquent plea for a balance between instruction that pushed concepts and instruction that supported traditional drills. Sensing that math education was in a state of flux, confused and worried parents in affluent areas began seeking out supplementary math instruction like Kumon, which focused on introducing a few math skills in an orderly sequence and providing students with endless opportunity for repetition. Kumon wasn't a panacea, but it was a partial antidote for an in-school math program whose goals were unclear. In the 1970s, Kumon consisted of a handful of storefronts in upscale neighborhoods in the Northeast. In 2008, there were 1,330 Kumon centers across the country. Even now, commonly used math textbooks continue to reflect the deep confusion about how to teach math.

On my desk are two of the most popular math textbooks used

in elementary and middle schools in this country. They are heavily illustrated. Both contain more than two hundred or so math concepts. Some of the topics seem unconnected from what came before. One textbook calls for teachers to teach units on whole numbers twice and the second time around presents what appears to be an almost random subunit called "climate comparisons." The language in the textbooks is often imprecise. It refers to "easy" addition facts and "harder" subtraction facts—and even non-mathematicians can tell you that dubbing information as "harder" doesn't exactly prime the pump for its smooth acquisition. In the early years, the guides suggest students do math-influenced art projects. Unfortunately, in many schools, these textbooks are teachers' instructional bibles.

Frustratingly, long-term trend data from the Nation's Report Card shows that for all the debate about the right way to teach math, teachers in the United States still aren't getting it right. In 1973, nine-year-olds scored 219 out of 500 on the NAEP. In 2008, their scores moved up to 243. Among thirteen-year-olds in the same time period, test scores moved up from 266 to 281. Seventeen-year-olds scored 304 in 1973. In 2008, their score was 306.

For the strength of our nation, we have to do better. But how?

MATH PROBLEMS MONKEYS CAN DO

I'm standing near a row of animal cages at a laboratory a short drive from Duke University trying not to inhale the pervasive scent of monkey urine. To get to the laboratory, I've navigated up a winding drive, made my way through a thick woods, and entered what looks like a summer camp surrounded by a chain-link fence topped by a length of more chain link—an effort to keep the primates in the compound and animal rights activists out.

But nothing painful or shocking is happening to the animals

here. In fact, the Duke Lemur Center is a little like Oxford for monkeys. Directly in front of me, a seventeen-pound monkey from Madagascar is standing on a plastic box in front of a touch screen that flashes green squares with different numbers of red dots inside. The monkey—a lemur actually—is estimating numbers. When he touches the square that has the greatest number of red dots, he gets a Splenda-seasoned pellet of food.

Lemurs are a shifty-looking species. To be fair, they don't all look alike. Some of them boast luxuriant coats in black, gray, and browns, while others have pelts that are patchy and moth-eaten. Still others have random shocks of red and orange on their heads, backs, or paws, making them look a little like mischievous teenagers right before Halloween. Almost all of them, though, have conspicuously beady eyes. Passing rows and rows of them in their spacious cages, I couldn't help but feel like they were holding back on expressing some malevolent opinions until their visitors were out of earshot. The way they move—more like opossums or raccoons than branch-to-branch swinging monkeys—doesn't make them seem any more trustworthy. And although their skulls are about the size of a clenched fist, these wily primates have a way with numbers.

In the last twenty years, scientists around the country have been trying to figure out just how animals think: what they perceive, what and how much they can hold in their memory, and how they make decisions. Dr. Elizabeth Brannon, a lean woman with an abundance of brown hair, has been involved in this research for about ten years and, along with others, has dedicated part of her research to figuring out how lemurs do math.

Doctoral candidate Sarah Jones hits a key on her portable computer keyboard and the experiment starts again. Two squares appear with different numbers of red dots. *Boink.* Aristides gets it right and gobbles down his pellet. To make sure the lemur isn't merely eyeballing the amount of red surface area present in each square, the size of the dots alternates: sometimes the lemur will have to choose between a square with three big red dots and a square that has five small dots.

Boink. The lemur touches the correct square and quickly gobbles down his pellet. More squares. He sniffs the touch screen, reaches out his strangely humanoid hand to touch the screen with the most dots. *Boink.* Another pellet. I crouch down to get eye level with the screen. Not only does the lemur appear to be estimating the number of dots correctly, he seems to be able to do it more quickly than I can. *Boink.* Beats me again.

"Since when have monkeys been able to do math?" I ask. Brannon corrects me. "We don't think they can actually do math," she says. Mathematics involves an interlocking series of complex mental processes that are tied up in our linguistic abilities, our ability to think abstractly, and our ability to understand representation. Lemurs can't do that. They wouldn't, she explains, "understand that the numeral 3 was a representation of three dots."

Since the early 1980s, though, scientists have been able to show that many kinds of animals, including rats, pigeons, and primates, have an approximate numbers sense. In experiments conducted over the years, Elizabeth Spelke, Rochel Gelman, Randy Gellistel, and many other scientists have shown that animals can discriminate among numbers up to a point, count, estimate, and figure proportion. Lemurs have this capacity in spades. Lemurs were isolated on a remote island in the middle of the Indian Ocean for about fifty million years. Natural selection, it seems, favored those who could choose a big bunch of bananas, say, over a smaller one. They developed a nose for numbers—ancient, evolutionary, and unlearned. Brannon and her graduate students, and scientists around the globe, are trying to figure out the limits of that numbers sense and determine if it can be developed into something more.

Later, in her sunny office, Brannon shows me a videotape of an earlier experiment she and her graduate student Jessica Cantion conducted, in which they taught a rhesus macaque (which looks like a big monkey or a small ape) to add. The macaque, which, to my consternation, is wearing a red bandana around his neck, watches a touch screen as three dots emerge from the right of the screen and travel to a square in the middle. Then four dots move from the top of the screen toward the middle square. When the four dots hit the middle square, it disappears and in a second, three squares are on the screen: one has five dots in it, one has two dots in it, and one has seven dots in it. The ape twists his head as if to get a look at all the squares, and then pushes the square that has seven dots in it.

Three dots plus four dots equal seven dots. He is rewarded with a sip of sweet juice from a spout near his head.

It turns out that children—even babies—have this gut numbers sense, too. In animals as in humans, it is controlled by a one-inch fold in the brain called the intraparietal sulcus, located approximately where you'd back-comb your hair if you wanted to create a beehive hairdo. And that little fold seems to be engaged and working hard almost from birth. In fact, in the middle 1980s, scientists from the University of Maryland found that newborns could discriminate between the numbers 2 and 3 a few days after birth.

Those discoveries flew directly in the face of that long-held conventional wisdom about kids and math. Children have math abilities early and far beyond what we once could have imagined. Over the years, though, scientists have debated what gut numbers sense is and isn't. For example, gut numbers sense is probably not a single system but an interaction of several systems in the brain. It has limits. A six-month-old baby can recognize that the quantity of four is larger than the quantity of one, but he can't tell the difference between one dot and five dots. Gut numbers sense doesn't allow babies (or lemurs) to count their fingers because counting relies on more complicated processes like knowing that the word *three* represents three dots but also that three is followed by the word *four*, which represents four. It does, however, allow animals and people to "see," at least in a rough way, the logic in simple addition, subtraction, division, and even rate. For a time, most scientists believed that these primitive systems were evolutionary tools—and nothing more. But some scientists speculated that these systems, while evolutionary in nature, might actually prime kids to learn math.

In 2008, Justin Halberda and a group of scientists from Johns Hopkins University made a stunning breakthrough that provided some of the strongest evidence yet that gut numbers sense plays a pivotal role in our ability to learn math. Halberda and his team started by rounding up sixty-four teenagers with whom they had worked previously (no mean feat in itself) and placed them before two screens. The researchers then flashed sets of between five and sixteen blue and yellow dots on the screens too quickly for them to count. The teens were asked to press a button and utter a verbal cue to indicate which screen they believed contained more dots. Would all adolescents have the same gut numbers sense strength? "We looked at individual kids and asked, is there a difference?" says Halberda. "The results were a screaming 'Yes!' Some kids had a highly precise representation of number and other kids struggled." And that variability shone through even after the researchers controlled for IQ and for difference is visual-spatial abilities.

This led Halberda and his team to a second and even more intriguing question: Do those differences tell us anything about how kids do in mathematics? Those weren't just random teenagers

Halberda tested. The team had measured each of those subjects' math ability and IQ since kindergarten. They found that their subjects' gut numbers sense at fourteen correlated almost perfectly with their performance in math throughout their early years of school.

Back in chapters 1 and 4 we saw how phonemic awareness undergirds reading ability. Is gut numbers sense the phonemic awareness for computation? "Undergird is a good way to describe it," says Halberda. "I don't want to call it math ability, since it's the same thing rats have. It isn't a formal system of mathematics, but it is related to our learning and our performance."

Halberda's study suggests that early numbers sense forms a kind of mental rebar for math skills.

Subsequent studies were done on large numbers of people—Halberda has tested the numbers sense of over fifty thousand subjects.* Using this large sample size, he has been able to show that while all children seem to have gut numbers sense, its intensity becomes defined at around age seven and strengthens until about age thirty. Numbers sense then begins to plateau in the middle years and begins to decline around sixty-five. The variation among individuals is astonishing—twelve-year-olds can have as strong a numbers sense as thirty-year-olds. And the reverse is also true.

The questions that are now obsessing Halberda and scientists around the globe are whether this skill predicts achievement, if it can be strengthened, and how. Halberda's big study suggests that the strength of our gut numbers sense changes over time, but is that variance a result of some deep and immutable neurological programming or is there some kind of instruction or something in culture

---

* If you want to be part of this experiment, go online to TestMyBrain.org or Panamath .org.

(square dancing? rapping? video games?) that can amplify it? If our underlying math sense strengthens like a muscle, when is the best time to start the training? In preschool? In elementary school? By college? Will the effects of the intervention be long-lasting? Should you try to intervene for kids who have a weak numbers sense or could all kids benefit from gut numbers sense training? If scientists come up with a way to make a kid's numbers sense get stronger, will it actually improve that child's ability to do math?

No one can answer those questions with certainty, at least not yet. "There is a huge wave of understanding about math cognition in cognitive psychology and neuroscience that is now beginning to crest," says Halberda. Serious scientists like Brannon and Halberda, though, say adapting these discoveries to the classroom will require intense collaboration with schools. "I'm absolutely not prepared to generate conjecture about how math teaching should be done," says Halberda. "I'm an expert in the science and cognition of mathematics." But when it comes to math instruction, he says he's "ready to be a listener to the teachers. How math should be taught is a rich and complicated problem."

Some schools and some teachers, though, have already found a way to use a kid's internal and innate math logic—their gut numbers sense or something close to it—to improve math achievement in the classroom.

BUILDING MATH SKILLS IN SCHOOL

Springhurst Elementary School in Dobbs Ferry, New York, is not the kind of place where you'd expect a radical departure from traditional instruction. It is part of a stable middle-class bedroom community of New York. The lawns are tidy and the streets, even during a winter with record snowfall, are well plowed. But inside the kindergarten through fifth-grade school, something revolutionary is going on with math instruction.

About three years ago, the then director of curriculum and instruction, Marjorie Holderman, got wind of some new ideas about teaching math. At Springhurst, though, math instruction was not a pressing problem. In general, the kids do just fine on both English and math standardized tests. Most students graduate from high school and go on to college. But the well-educated parents in Dobbs Ferry are demanding. They'd long complained about a math curriculum that is a mile wide and an inch thick, says Holderman. Besides, as at every high-functioning school, the staff at Dobbs Ferry are "always looking to improve, to make our practice better."

Their math program is based on a nearly five-decades-old system used in Singapore. In 1965, determined to develop a more educated population, the education ministry in Singapore rejected Piaget's notions of kids "growing into math" and developed a program based on the ideas of another developmental psychologist, an American named Jerome Bruner, who argued that kids are capable of learning nearly any material so long as it is organized, sequenced, and represented in a way they can understand. By the late 1980s, when Singapore began dominating the international benchmark tests in math, affluent and well-traveled parents began begging their expat friends to send them Singapore math textbooks. In the last couple of years, the Singapore textbooks and material have been adapted for an American audience.

The program is a radical departure from what most American kids are used to. At a time when parents think good math instruction is accompanied by worksheets, Singapore math demands that students understand math, not simply perform math functions. The textbooks are very thin. There are no pizzas in slices or assignments to journal about numbers. In the early years of elementary school, children are given manipulatives like specially developed bars and coins and grouping frames to help make an organizing concept like *base ten* more visual and more concrete. There is no repetitive drilling on algorithms. No pages with fifty two-digit addition and subtraction problems. The idea is that if you understand the information the algorithm is conveying, you don't have to solve it by rote memory. You don't have to remember the "rules." The answer is something that makes sense based on what you have been taught about numbers. And, especially in the early years of Singapore math instruction, that instruction about numbers constantly pulls from a student's innate sense of math logic. It's conceptual math on steroids.

Not long ago, Frank Ferri kicked off his a fifth-grade math class with a word problem:

> A farmer plowed 8⅛ acres one day, 2⅔ acres the next morning, and 3⅝ acres on the afternoon of the second day.

Briefly, the class discussed what information they could gain from the facts that were presented. Mr. Ferri wrote down each suggestion. Then they figured out which ones were mathematically valid. Then they began solving a problem suggested by one of the students: How many acres did the farmer plow altogether?

The entire class worked together and came up with different ways to solve the equations. But this is no "There Are No Wrong Answers" type of math class. Each time a child suggested a different path, he was required to explain the structure and patterns he perceived that governed his solution. The students have been taught to use the language of math correctly. Miles, a short-haired boy in a striped T-shirt, took a good long time to formulate his answer. Mr. Ferri waited and so did the class. When he finally was able to articulate his thoughts, his language was precise. When a child's thinking is flawed, being required to explain it out loud—to make sense of it to his classmates—usually highlights the problem.

Yes, these kids learn math facts like multiplication tables. Those are considered fundamental. Proponents of this method believe that math instruction that depends on memorizing math facts and executing algorithms—the kind of math education most of our children get in schools today—without conceptual understanding is like learning a foreign language without ever hearing it spoken. You may be able to read a menu or even read a simple tabloid news story. But unless your ear becomes attuned to aural signals that create the language, you'll never fully grasp its power or its lyricism.

Singapore-style math was developed thirty years ago, long before the scientific discoveries about gut numbers sense began to reach a crescendo. But what is fascinating about the program is the way that it acknowledges and promotes a child's instinctual ability to size up the meaning of numbers.

"Children have these skills," says Josh Rosen, Springhurst's math specialist. "When we ask them to solve equations, that's what they bring to the table. Their own ways of looking at numbers. This program asks teachers to honor that thinking." And use it as a tool to move them into higher-order mathematics.

It is challenging to teach math this way. Elementary and middle school math teachers are trained to be generalists, not math specialists. When they teach math, they tend to use the highly scripted teaching guide that comes with a textbook as a lesson plan. Singapore-style math is about seeing numbers in a broader way. And that leaves the gap in a teacher's math knowledge more exposed.

After the fifth-grade class was finished, Frank Ferri explained how challenging this kind of teaching can be. As a longtime elementary school educator, he's highly skilled in instruction, but he's brave enough to admit that like many of us, his math skills are limited. "When we ask kids to think about the meaning of math, some of their ideas go very deep. And it can be unnerving. I might know the math they are thinking about, but do I know it well enough to teach it?" During the word problem about the farmer, one of his students suggested they determine the average of acres plowed per session. The instruction was about adding fractions. "Dividing improper fractions," said Ferri. "Well, I had to think, Do I know that?"

Rosen, the Singapore math guru at Springhurst, has begun an in-house class for elementary school teachers to improve their knowledge of math and improve their fluency. "The more math they know, the more risks they are willing to take," said Rosen. The more they know, the better than can teach.

In his 1997 book *The Number Sense: How the Mind Creates Mathematics*, Stanislas Dehaene, one of the pioneers of the neurocognitive exploration of our math ability, argues that formal education needs to align better with how humans learn math. "Most children enter preschool with a well-developed understanding of approximation and counting. In most courses, this informal baggage is treated as a handicap rather than an asset." Good schooling, he writes, "plays a crucial role not so much because it teaches children new arithmetic techniques, but also because it helps them draw links between the mechanics of good calculation and its meaning. . . . The flame of mathematical intuition is only flickering in a child's mind; it needs to be fortified and sustained before it can illuminate all arithmetic activities." He wasn't talking about the math program at Dobbs Ferry, but he might have been.

So far, the parents in Dobbs Ferry have been supportive of the program. The school does a great deal of outreach. Rosen has been holding a "Math Education Night" to teach parents how to best support this new kind of instruction at home. Not long ago, he found himself explaining to a group of three parents, all engineers, how the distributive property is introduced as a tool to solve math problems. "They were nodding along and saying, yes, yes, this is a scaled-down version of how we think of math in our work." And that, said Rosen, was an important endorsement.

WHAT YOUR CHILD NEEDS

Unfortunately, while scientists are limning the precursors of math ability in babies—and innovative administrators and teachers are talking about how to enhance it in all kids—many preschool and early primary school teachers go out of their way to minimize math instruction. If you spend any time touring preschools and kindergartens, it is possible to be in classrooms that have virtually no math materials beyond a few numbers posted up along with letters.

In part, many teachers hold on to Piaget's idea that children need to "grow into" abstract thinking. But now research suggests that children often don't know math at an early age not because they are not developmentally ready for it but because they haven't been exposed to it. What children are "ready for" is largely contingent on prior opportunities to learn. In general, early experience with numbers and quantity at home builds into early math learning, which sets the stage for more math.

In elementary school, math instruction takes center stage. But it is often math instruction of the worst kind. Many elementary school teachers cling to poorly organized math textbooks the way drowning men cling to buoys. Which reflects another issue that may be depressing math achievement: primary school teachers are often secret mathphobes. In a presentation given to the American Educational Research Association in 2010, two doctoral students from Columbia University's Teachers College surveyed novice teachers' level of math anxiety. It was not very encouraging. Responses included apathy ("I'm not really a math person") to near phobia ("To this day, I get nervous if I have to do any simple math without the aid of a calculator") to something akin to post-traumatic stress disorder resulting from early math trauma ("I decided that I hate math and, essentially, forever blocked any interest in seriously attempting to understand or learn mathematics in any way, shape, or form.") Teachers who embrace math will ensure that it has a big place in their classroom and work double-time to make certain that students connect math to all aspects of daily life.

Clues? Your child should be getting more than math worksheets. Early on, look for "math manipulatives," which are often the chips, blocks, and rods teachers use to visually reinforce the idea of concepts. Look for number lines. Much should be made of quantity and measurement. Ask for a curriculum that goes beyond math "practice"—learning math facts and executing algorithms. Singapore-style math isn't the only way, but good instruction uses and enhances what children already know.

Keep a sharp and critical eye on your child's math textbook. If your child's school is mired in old-style math instruction, the textbook will be massive. It may be a great program, or teachers who don't know much math themselves may be presenting a confused, overbroad curriculum. Find out what is happening. You may need to supplement your child's math education. There are several organizations that sell Singapore-style math textbooks—and even individual math lessons—to parents.

Your interest and enthusiasm for math achievement matter. It turns out that the attitudes you hold toward math instruction and what you as parents express to your children can have a massive impact on their achievement.

WHAT YOU SAY ABOUT MATH MATTERS

Elite colleges in the United States enroll a lot of Asian kids. Right now, Asians make up only 5 percent of the general population of our country and at the same time make up 18 percent of the student population at Harvard, 24 percent at Stanford, and 27 percent at MIT. Asian American civil rights activists say those numbers would be even higher if it weren't for anti-Asian discrimination routinely practiced by private universities that are trying to keep an informal cap on the proportion of Asian American students on their campuses.

Indeed, in California, where the state college system is prevented by law from discriminating on the basis of ethnicity, Asian students rule. Asians, who make up 12 percent of the population of the state, make up an astonishing 46 percent of the student population at highly prestigious UC Berkeley and competitive UC Davis, and 56 percent of the student population at UC Irvine.

If you are a culturally sensitive person, you are probably rolling your eyes right now. When we talk about Asian Americans we lump together people from many different countries and ethnic backgrounds. The stereotype of Asians as America's "model minority" is a crude one: to be sure, Asian American enclaves have the same array of social problems as every other subcategory of American citizens. But the undeniable fact is that more Asian American kids do better at math than any other ethnic group on our shores.

In 2009, according to the Nation's Report Card, math scores for Asian kids in fourth grade were 255 (on a 500-point scale), while white and black kids trailed at 248 and 222, respectively. In eighth grade, math scores for Asian kids were 300, while white kids got a 292 and black kids 260.

When pressed, Asian community leaders say their kids do well in school because Asian parents make education the family's number one priority. But plenty of parents put their kids' schooling first—and get lesser results. Especially when it comes to math. It seems politically incorrect to pose the question, but here goes: Is there something about being Asian that could be providing kids with an advantage in math?

Turns out, about ten years ago, a network of social scientists led by two renowned psychologists—the late Harold Stevenson from the University of Michigan and James W. Stigler, a professor at UCLA—spent several years trying to come up with an answer to that exact question. They conducted a series of elegantly designed international studies in China, Japan, Taiwan, and the United States, trying to identify what it is about Asian cultures—was it innate intelligence, schooling, or family attitudes?—that primed their children for success in math. Their conclusion should change the way you think about math education—and help your kids do better.

The first studies pinpointed the achievement difference. And it is staggering. Japanese children perform better than American children, even in kindergarten. And the magnitude of that difference increases every year kids are at school. The Asian Advantage is not limited to the performance of children in highly industrialized nations, like Japan. Children in undeveloped swaths of mainland China outperform their counterparts in suburban United States. The researchers then tried to answer this question: Could something about being East Asian—perhaps a genetic trait—be making kids smarter? This is a very delicate question to ask. Most people in the scientific community don't look at intelligence as a fixed inborn characteristic but rather as a quality that is subject to the complex interaction between nature and nurture. However, the scientists reasoned, perhaps the ancient ancestors of modern-day Asians faced evolutionary pressures that favored the selection of particular cognitive abilities. Perhaps they had developed a super math gene.

So Stevenson and Stigler tested East Asian kids and kids from the United States on several measures: intelligence, vocabulary and word comprehension, visual spatial abilities—skills that had been associated with math ability and solving word problems—and, separately, their math ability. Then they compared the results.

After starting off behind on measures of intelligence, school-age Asian kids tested slightly higher than kids of European descent later on. On tests measuring verbal ability, Asian kids were slightly behind kids of European descent, but the difference between the two groups faded by age ten. From age five, Asian kids scored consistently higher than kids of European descent on measures of visual spatial skills, starting in the early years, and continued to dominate all through school. It was a mixed picture.

As the scientists were working over the numbers, they turned up some very interesting data. As expected, there was a correlation between intelligence and math ability: kids in all the countries who scored in the top range on IQ tests tended to do better at math. But the range of math achievement scores for smart kids varied a great deal from country to country. A Japanese child of average intelligence compared to other Japanese children showed average math abilities. When scientists compared that average Japanese child to his American counterpart—an American child of average intelligence—the average Japanese child's math abilities put him near the top of the American class. Conversely, American children of average intelligence with average math scores were at the bottom quartile of the range of Japanese kids' math achievement. Those scientists uncovered in stark terms what the researchers like Stanford economist Eric Hanushek have pointed out again and again: in our homes and in our schools, we are failing to realize the potential of what should be top American children.

What could be behind this achievement gap? Obviously, schooling is a big factor. It stands to reason that kids who attended highly effective schools and who were taught by master teachers would do better. But there was more to it than that—Stevenson and Stigler tested seven thousand children and the schools they attended were highly variable.

So the scientists began probing other factors that might contribute to the Asian Advantage. They began interviewing hundreds of students and their moms in Asian and American cities. What they found is this: Americans, more than any other people, attribute success in mathematics to innate ability rather than hard work. When asked to weight the four factors—effort, ability, task difficulty, and luck—that contributed to success on a math test, Japanese and Taiwanese mothers pointed to effort. American mothers pointed to natural ability. American mothers strongly disagreed with the statement, "People tend to have the same amount of math ability" and in another part of the questionnaire tended to agree with the statement, "Your child is born with his/her math ability." Few Japanese and Taiwanese mothers endorsed that sentiment. American moms tended to believe that their child's math ability asserted itself early or not at all. More than a third of American mothers but only 10 percent of Chinese mothers believed you could make an accurate prediction about a child's performance in math in high school by their abilities at the end of fifth grade.

What is holding American kids back in mathematics? Poorly

conceived curriculum and dumbed-down textbooks might be part of it. But parents bear responsibility for the underachievement of their children, too. What we've learned from Justin Halberda is that the strength and precision of guts numbers sense is variable. But we can help our children do the most with what they have. In the United States, parents believe math is a talent or a gift, like a clear sweet soprano singing voice—and in that way they discourage children from expending a great deal of effort to master the material, in the same way you might steer your uncoordinated child away from traveling soccer team tryouts. But in East Asian countries, parents tell their children in a hundred different ways that math ability is a muscle that can be built over time—provided they work at it.

Researchers who study mathematical instruction and achievement in the United States say it's high time that American parents got real about what it takes to help kids do better in math. Developmental psychologist David Geary, a professor at the University of Missouri, is the lead investigator on a longitudinal study designed to track children's mathematical development and learning disabilities around math. He also served as an adviser to the federal government on math education. He says part of the problem in American schools lies in the misguided efforts by some curriculum writers and educators to not only connect math to real life but, along the way, suggest that math can be whimsical, amusing, or entertaining. Primary and middle school teachers, he says, "want students to believe that math is fun. But what mathematicians tell us is that early on, when kids are laying down the foundations of higher math, it isn't fun. It takes work. Hard work."

He advises teacher and parents to tell it to kids straight. Being good at math is not based on talent. It's work. But it's worth it. The more opportunities you have to do math, and the more effort you expend, the better you'll get at it.

THE TAKE AWAYS

1. Talk about math ideas from the time your child is small. Help those ideas grow. Keep it informal and conversational: bigger than or smaller than, more or less, counting— even adding and subtracting.

2. Preschool and kindergarten teachers should spend some part of the day working deeply and purposefully with math ideas. They should be talking about math concepts. By first grade, children should be starting to work with math problems as an extension of understanding the meaning of math problems.

3. When it comes to elementary school math, look for a scaled-down curriculum that moves forward in an orderly and coherent way.

4. Your attitude counts. Repeat after me: Math is not a talent. Being good at math is a product of hard work. The harder you work, the better you will be.

CHAPTER SIX

THE RIGHT BALANCE

THERE ARE MANY things that Norman Boldt, a stay-at-home dad, likes about the public elementary school in his Florida neighborhood. Both of his children were eligible for gifted programs and the school, which serves the affluent neighborhood just outside of Miami where he lives, has provided good instruction to accommodate their academic needs. The teachers are thoughtful and caring and the principal, who arrived shortly after Boldt's older son moved up to middle school, is intelligent and welcoming. But when the couple's younger son, Matthew, was in first grade, Boldt noticed that the school day seemed to take a lot out of him. When Boldt picked him up at three o'clock he often seemed glazed over in a way that is unusual for an active and inquisitive seven-year-old. A frequent visitor and regular volunteer at the school, Boldt had always noted with approval that the school was clean and well-maintained. He never saw the gymnasium, but then again, he had never looked. Now, for the first time, he realized that the school didn't have a gymnasium where kids could regularly attend a physical education class. And besides, PE was only scheduled for two or three times a week. As for recess? Well, the school had a playing field and an outdoor basketball court, but it occurred to Boldt that he hadn't seen kids using it much. He began to talk to other parents. "I realized that they were in class from eight thirty to three and the kids weren't getting any breaks in the school day," says Boldt. "I really think the students do need a break. They need to get outside. There is not time for them to unwind."

So he spoke to the principal. "The principal told me that there is not much you can do," Boldt explains. "There were mandates that kids have so many minutes a week of instructional time in so many subjects." The kids were on a block schedule—a scheduling plan for the day that extends each subject period and is supposed to give teachers time for deeper lessons. But those "blocks" create less flexible school days for children. "The principal said when it got added all together, there are no minutes left." Boldt makes sure to schedule some outdoor play for his sons soon after the school day ends. "They come out of that class looking like zombies," he says. "Honestly, a day without breaks can't be good."

Few issues strike parents as being more important than the scheduling of the school day. While we recognize that education is a complicated business, most of us have strong opinions about how to arrange a day to get the best out of our child. We've learned—sometimes by painful missteps—that letting our kids run around bolsters their ability to sit still. Small breaks for snacks, socializing, and spacing out can improve their focus, but too much distraction can reduce their ability to stick with a task. We expect that school administrators, who share our desire to get the best out of our kids, will keep these issues in mind. Most of us also assume that our schools will be providing our children with a well-rounded education—giving them academic skills like mathematics and reading but also teaching them enough science, history, civics, art, and music so they will be prepared for work or college and, above all, to become citizens in a democratic society. And often they are. But sometimes, for reasons we'll look at in this chapter, school administrators make decisions about the school day that seem at odds with those goals—and can leave us scratching our heads in bewilderment and our kids fidgeting with frustration.

In many parts of the country, the traditional school schedule—which in our lifetimes has been comprised of 180 or so 6.5-hour school days that start in the fall and end in the spring—is being reexamined and remade. Last year, Minnesota's school superintendents proposed increasing the school year from 175 to 200 days. A business-led group in Delaware is proposing state funding for an additional 140 school hours a year as a part of its plan for improving the state's education system. A group of Illinois legislators have proposed extending the school year in schools throughout the state. New Mexico governor Bill Richardson recently proposed a longer school day and year for low-performing schools. And Massachusetts's lawmakers included $6.5 million in the state budget to support a public-private partnership to expand learning time for ten schools in five districts. Some high-profile charter schools such as KIPP (Knowledge Is Power Program), which serves low-income kids in twenty states, have tacked on an extra three weeks of summer instruction and mandatory four-hour Saturday sessions. In the fall of 2010, President Obama called for longer days and shorter summer vacations. The school day, which once seemed like a fixed pattern of fifty-five-minute classes broken up by snack, recess, and lunch, is changing.

In our test-driven schools, the notion that "what gets tested, gets taught" has placed reading and math instruction front and center, whereas time for social studies, science, art, music, and PE has been reduced. Recess, which many elementary school children once described as the best part of the school day, is being whittled away or used as a reward for hard work instead of a regularly scheduled break. In many schools, recess—which was long a time of unstructured free play—has become yet another highly structured, goal-oriented, and adult-led activity.

How much schooling does your child need? Is there an advantage to keeping your child in school later or sending him to school year-round? What is the right balance of instruction and breaks? Does your child need recess, and if so, how much? And what about PE? Some of these questions have very solid answers. For others, compelling research is only now beginning to emerge.

ONE HUNDRED AND EIGHTY DAYS

Although it seems like the school calendar has always been configured the same way, in fact, around the country, the length of the day and the year has varied a great deal in the last 150 years—and the amount of time kids went to school depended on where their parents lived. Schools in rural communities, where the rhythms of life revolved around agriculture, had the shortest school year, allowing kids plenty of time to fulfill their responsibilities at home, on the farm, and in the field. By contrast, in the 1840s, school systems in major cities like Buffalo, Detroit, and Philadelphia were open 251 to 260 days a year. In New York City, schools were open nearly year-round with only a three-week break in August. By the turn of the century, families that had accumulated some wealth wanted to take their kids away from the heat (and rampant disease) of the city during the summer and lobbied for a longer summer break. At the end of the nineteenth century, most urban schools observed a two-month-long summer holiday. Recognizing that farm-raised children would have to compete for jobs with city-raised kids, rural communities lengthened their calendars to keep up. By 1900, the nation's schools were open an average of 144 days.

During the early twentieth century, as immigration spiked, many cities started year-round schools again in order to teach the recently arrived youth to speak English well enough to get a job.

Around that time, a group of business leaders, supported by industrialist and philanthropist Andrew Carnegie, decided that high school education—especially a college preparatory education—was entirely too haphazard. To standardize it, they proposed a time-based system for measuring educational attainment—120 hours of class time or contact with a teacher—which the group, ever-mindful of who was picking up the check for their work, dubbed the Carnegie unit. Then they asked colleges and universities around the country to assess applicants on whether or not they had attained enough Carnegie units. The colleges and universities squawked at being bossed around by the business community until the business community offered to improve their pensions in exchange for their adoption of the system. Opposition crumbled. Colleges began to evaluate high schoolers by the number of Carnegie units obtained. By 1910, nearly all American high schools had adopted the Carnegie unit measurement—and that unit of measurement trickled down to middle and late elementary school.

As Elena Silva describes in her paper, "On the Clock: Rethinking the Way Schools Use Time," the structure of the school day, though, was still not fixed in stone. When women were pressed into the workforce by the changing economy during World War II, public schools responded by offering extended-day school programs. By the 1960s, though, most schools in the country had settled on a schedule of 170 to 180 days, five days a week, six and a half hours a day. And that has remained the standard.

LOOKING ABROAD AND FEELING STUPID

By the early 1980s, educational policy makers began to grumble that kids weren't spending enough time in school. The famous 1983 report "A Nation at Risk" compared U.S. schools to Japanese schools and found that that U.S. kids were in school much less. Japan, at that time, seemed about to become what China and India are today: a newly emergent economy on the verge of overtaking our own. Some superintendents began experimenting with longer school years but it was expensive: union contracts for teachers, administrators, and janitors were devised around the 180-day school year. It was also unpopular with middle-class parents who argued that the halcyon days of summer provided valuable opportunities for their children to refuel and participate in other, nonacademic-type activities.

The drumbeat for a longer school year got louder in 1996, when Harris Cooper, a professor of education at Duke University, published a study on the effects of summer vacation. Cooper and his colleagues looked at thirty-five research studies and determined that, contrary to what parents might think, kids didn't put their minds on hold while they spent a summer climbing trees and chasing frogs. In fact, they experienced a kind of academic amnesia— their achievement levels didn't flatline but dipped. Cooper found kids lost about a month of learning during each standard summer vacation. The academic amnesia was more pronounced in kids from low-income families who, the researchers speculated, didn't spend as much time engaged in enriching activities. As a country, policy makers had been grappling with the achievement gap between poor and middle-class kids for years and there was still no good solution in sight. Summer vacation, the two months of freedom, the object of almost palpable yearning on the first warm spring day in any classroom in any state in the union, turned out to be hurting our kids—especially our disadvantaged kids.

Around that time, more data began to emerge that compared the achievement of U.S. schoolchildren with their counterparts in other developed nations. In study after study, the United States was falling behind. What did high-performing countries like Belgium and France have in common? The children there attended school for longer days or more overall days than American kids did.

In the last decade or so, school districts have begun experimenting with lengthening the school year again in earnest. It seemed like such a simple and obvious thing to change. As you may sense, though, education reform never turns out to be as easy as it should be. How much you spend on educating a kid—and how much time you spend doing it—are two of the most concrete, and controllable, inputs. Tinkering with the school day or the school year has become to education reformers what catnip is to cats: irresistible. But does making a school day or a school year longer actually help? The answer is complicated.

MORE TIME TO WASTE

Do children do better if they spend more time in school? Overall, the answer is yes, but maybe not quite as resounding and uniform a yes as we might think. And the kids who will be helped with more time in school will only gain that advantage if the additional school time is spent in the right way. Some social scientists, and particularly economists, can provide the kind of information about education that satellites provide to the Weather Channel: the really Big Picture. In a study released in 2010, Victor Lavy, an economics professor at Hebrew University and the University of London, did just that. He noted, like everyone else who's looked at this issue, that there are large differences in instructional time in different countries. He wanted to know if the amount of time a teacher spent talking could account for the different level of achievement by schoolkids in those countries. There are large discrepancies: fifteen-year-olds from Belgium, France, and Greece average about 1,000 hours per year of compulsory classroom instruction whereas similar-aged schoolkids in England and Sweden get only about 750 hours. Eleven-year-olds from Portugal get about 800 hours of instruction a year, and seven-year-olds in Finland get less than 600 hours. Lavy set out to determine on a grand scale whether the schoolchildren who got the most instructional time did better on tests in reading, math, and science. On a day-to-day basis, successful teaching and learning often hinge on minute details As we discussed in chapter 2 on testing, even when the teaching is top drawer, children can be distracted. Did the children have breakfast or are they listening to their stomachs growl? Are they quaking with self-consciousness about the tiny little muffin top created by their expensive new jeans? Did they get enough sleep last night? But crunching huge amounts of data can provide us with wide trend lines that transcend those quotidian concerns. Lavy looked at instructional hours from fifty different countries and then looked at test scores for a representative sample of kids from each place. Working an economist's voodoo on the numbers, he made his determination. In developed countries, adding one hour of instruction per week in math, science, or reading raises the test score in these subjects, but not by much. The improvement is more significant for girls, for pupils from poor families (particularly families who were not well grounded in reading), and for immigrants.

So why not extend school days for all kids, thereby providing them with more instructional time? Remember, the answer is more complicated than the question. It turns out that extending the school day doesn't necessarily expand instructional time.

You are probably scratching your head right now, wondering how the day could get longer while the amount of instruction remains the same size. Here's what researchers have found. As you have probably surmised by now, educational practices are being studied from every direction and from every angle. In the late 1980s, time management experts got hold of ten years' worth of surveys. Between 1976 and 1986, second- through fifth-grade math and reading teachers had described, among other things, their typical day. They found that in a large number of American public schools, a huge chunk of the school day was taken up with activities like lunch, recess, school assemblies, and activities that had only a peripheral relationship to actual learning. Another chunk was taken up with classroom administrative-type activities like roll call, discipline, and announcements coming over the PA system. One researcher, pulling data from the study, determined that children were actually engaged in learning less than 38 percent of the day.

Sometimes it's even worse. In 1998, the prestigious Consortium on Chicago Schools Research took a hard look at just how much time elementary schools in Chicago were actually spending on educating children. At the time, Chicago public schools were required to be open 180 days a year and operated for five and a half hours a day. Out of those 330 minutes in a day, teachers were required to spend 300 minutes on instruction—900 hours a year. The schools' schedules were arranged for maximum efficiency—"language arts" were given 90 minutes or more each day, and there was not much time for lunch, study hall, or socializing. Gym, recess, art, and music were all but abandoned. After the Consortium researchers spent months in the schools, then returned to tabulate their data, they got a shock. They were aware that the school schedule seemed anything but lax, but when everything was added up, the children in Chicago public schools, which were among the nation's worst, were getting somewhere on the order of 500 hours of instruction a year—nowhere near the 900 hours required by the district. The school day was taken up with discipline, assemblies, bake sales, computer lab, cutting animals out of magazines for book covers, read-alouds, holiday celebrations, test preparation, test taking, and awards ceremonies.

READING AND MATH BOOT CAMP

Armed with the research connecting what is called "time on task" with performance, many schools—especially schools where kids are struggling—have shifted their schedules so that the vast majority of the day is taken up with reading and math. And no wonder: a student's performance on standardized tests in these subjects determines the reputation of the school and the autonomy of the administration and teachers. Even a modest boost can help a school's reputation and allow the people in school leadership roles to keep their jobs.

For several years, people who believe in a holistic approach to education and families with a strong connection to the arts have decried the narrowing of the curriculum and criticized those back-to-basics schools, which emphasize only reading and math (the subjects that get tested). Many have worried publicly that less time is being given to music, visual art, and dance—to the detriment of children. How much the curriculum is actually being narrowed is a matter of great debate, and good research points in two directions. In 2006, a survey by the nonpartisan Center on Education Policy examined 299 school districts in all fifty states to determine, in part, the fallout from No Child Left Behind testing requirements. Researchers there estimated that a full 71 percent of the nation's 15,000 school districts had reduced the hours of instructional time of history, music, and art. "Narrowing the curriculum has clearly become a nationwide pattern," Jack Jennings, CEP's president, told the *New York Times* when the report was released.

Since then, though, research has cast doubt on those findings: in February 2009, the Government Accountability Office, the investigative arm of Congress, combed through federal survey data and found that teachers reported that instructional time devoted to the arts had remained about the same between 2004 (when the effects of NCLB were really starting to dawn on schools) and the 2006–7 school year. Unlike the CEP report, which found nearly three out of four schools reducing arts instruction, their data indicated something different. Four percent of schools reported an increase in time devoted to teaching dance, visual arts, and music. Seven percent of schools reported a drop in instructional time for the arts—and most of those schools are attended by minority kids who are struggling to meet state standards.

Anecdotally, education reporters, principals, teachers, and parents say "back to basics" schools—ones where the day is given over to math and reading instruction—are common. Schools in poor communities are driven by assessment. Kids are assessed on math and reading. As former secretary of education Margaret Spellings was fond of saying, "What gets tested, gets taught."

Since the GOA's report was issued, though, school curriculums have narrowed for another reason: budget cuts. And nobody at any level of government seems to be denying it. States, struggling with massive deficits, have slashed funding to schools, which in turn are cutting staff. First to go? Teachers who provide instruction in subjects that aren't getting tested.

In the last eighteen months, Anna-Lise Pasch Santella, a musicology doctoral student at the University of Chicago, and her husband, Andrew, a writer, have watched the curriculum in their son's elementary school in Cary, Illinois, go from being what they would describe as enriched to something much more basic and infinitely less appealing.

Their town, an exurb about ninety minutes drive from Chicago, has been particularly hard hit by the recession. Plummeting property values, stalled development, a dearth of new families moving in, and high unemployment have led to the district closing two schools and firing about a third of all the teachers. The gifted program? Gone. Science instruction, art, music, and gym, too, have all been curtailed.

The librarians were let go, and while a clerk keeps the library open, the school can't afford to buy books or replace ones that get ripped or dirty. Parents are trying to step in, volunteering during the school day and launching projects in the now-forgotten subjects. Meanwhile, to the dismay of the Santellas, the annual standardized testing is now a thrice-yearly affair. "We've thought about private school," says Anna-Lise, "but if we do that, we will not be able to afford any of the other enriching after-school activities that our son enjoys." She and her husband have begun to supplement their son's learning at home, but there are many families in their community who do not have the resources for art supplies and language lessons.

Does it matter? You'd be hard-pressed to find anyone connected with education who believes that history and science instruction are a luxury. Policy makers thinking about the skills children will need in the coming decades put science—and a second language—near the top of the list.

But what about arts? Do kids actually learn better when they learn to play the trombone, sing in the choir, interpret zoo animals in modern dance, or paint a self-portrait in blue—à la van Gogh? Anna-Lise says in her experience, the answer is a resounding yes. "I'm a musician, a violinist. For me, the way I got into everything I learned was through music. I learned languages—French and German—because I wanted to sing French and German lyrics. It gave me an access point."

Anna-Lise's feelings are echoed by many parents who strive to send their children to schools that provide opportunities to sample a wide variety of arts experiences. While that attitude makes sense, there is little data that directly links arts curriculum to improved academic learning. The same GAO report combed through about fifteen years of data on arts education and improved learning outcomes. Here's what they discovered: some studies show a small positive association between arts education and student academic achievement—in particular between learning to play music and math test scores. (The subjects were preschoolers up through fifth graders who had studied instrumental and voice performance for between four months and two years.) But others studies looking at the connection between music and math have found none. Is there some way that dance, music, and visual arts could improve scores in reading? It makes sense that those experiences give children a wider vocabulary and range of life experience that they can recognize in reading and reflect on in writing. Not all learning can be quantified in test scores. And speaking personally, I want them for my child. My view is that formal education should be aimed at maximizing academic learning, but it should also ground children in the culture and introduce them to pursuits that can give texture and meaning to our lives. As of this writing, though, the research connecting those pursuits to improved school achievement simply isn't there.

Teachers say that an enriched curriculum—one with plenty of history, science, arts, music, and dance—is the best way to keep all kinds of kids on track at school. The middle school in a middle-class section of the Bronx where English teacher Michael Duque worked for the last two years billed itself as a specialized-learning environment for kids who were interested in dance. Instead, Duque found it was a test prep boot camp. The reading and math scores were poor—only 21 percent of kids were proficient in English language arts and 28 percent of kids were proficient in math. So the curriculum revolved around almost nothing else. Three times a week, the children were given an hour and a half of reading and writing and an hour and a half of math. Twice a week, they were pulled from history or science and given an extra forty-five minutes of reading and writing. Children who had learning disabilities, kids who required speech therapy, and kids for whom English was a second language got additional instruction in reading and writing. The science and history teachers complained that children got pulled out for more intensive focus on reading and math so frequently that it was impossible for them to pass tests in those subjects. Children whose scores tended to skew low were "invited" to attend an extended-day program where, before or after school, they got another thirty-five minutes of reading and writing instruction. At the end of each day, kids were given a quick assessment similar to the ones that would be on the standardized test. Those who didn't score well enough were taught the same lesson the next day. Amazingly, never, in all that time devoted to reading and writing, was Duque allowed to read and discuss a full book with the children— only parts of a book.

Four times a week, the children who could dance were given dance, though there was no stage or auditorium. The rest of the kids, the ones who were admitted, not for their interest in dance but because there was no other school for them to attend, were allowed to take an art class. During the day, there was no physical education, no chorus, band, instrument playing, or music. One of the teachers got a grant to put on a play, but administrators wouldn't pay her extra for meeting with the children to rehearse.

"I often thought of my own education—in middle school in and high school," said Duque, who attended a public high school in Florida, "and how enriched it was with student council and theater and music. I felt really disheartened to see what the children were getting." At the end of the 2010 school year, Duque quit and found a job at a school where he didn't feel like the curriculum worked against the education of the children.

THE END OF RECESS

Nothing seems to bother parents more than when their kids are denied sufficient amounts of unstructured recess. Last fall, the principal at an upper-middle-class elementary school in Woodland Hills, California, almost had an insurrection on her hands when she instituted a new recess policy: the children would no longer be allowed to choose their activity or form mixed-aged groups. Instead, they were required to remain with their class and each day participate in a different adult-chosen activity—climbing, running track, socializing with classmates on the benches, or playing kickball.

A handful of concerned parents sought out a meeting with the principal and complained that the new system robbed children of opportunities to make choices and socialize freely. In response, the principal explained that the new system was designed to give teachers an opportunity to reinforce the content from the day's lessons. "During recess?" sputtered Lorin Engquist, whose son attends school there. "There are many parents who are concerned that their children just aren't getting their breaks. They need some opportunity during the school day to do what they want!"

The principal was unmoved. The policy stayed in place. Parents began bombarding the district office with complaints. (The Los Angeles Unified School District, where the school is located, has a clear policy supporting unstructured recess.) "The principal told us that we should not second-guess her decision about recess because she has a Ph.D. in education," says Engquist. "But as a friend of mine pointed out, he has a Ph.D. in raising his kid!"

Are the parents right? Do kids need unstructured recess time? How much and what kind? For decades, recess was a mainstay of the school experience. About fifteen years ago, recess and physical education lost their luster. As "time on task" became the school mantra, kids began spending more and more time indoors, seated at their desks. How much recess has been curtailed is a matter of debate. According to data collected by the Department of Education, 83 to 88 percent of elementary school kids have recess. But if you've ever stepped inside an elementary school, those percentages seem very high. What is irrefutable, though, is that rates of childhood obesity and diabetes are rising dramatically. So are attention issues. According to a 2010 report from the Centers for Disease Control and Prevention, the number of ADHD (attention deficit/hyperactivity disorder) cases in children jumped by 22 percent between 2003 and 2007—an increase of about one million kids. For a time, parents who questioned whether their children needed more physical movement during the day were seen as antiacademic. In the last five years, though, the scientific community has stepped in to support what for many parents seemed like common sense.

Recess, it turns out, is essential to education. Kids—just like adults—need movement in order to function at their cognitive peak. In 2001, when she was a pediatric resident, Dr. Romina Barros was given an assignment to shadow a high-functioning autistic child who was in the care of Brookdale Hospital where she worked. The child attended a local public school. Teachers there were complaining that the child was restless in class and the clinicians were wondering what was going on. "It was a first-grade classroom in the winter," recalls Barros. "And I was shocked to see that between early morning—when class began—and lunchtime, the children did not get a break. Even snack time was not a time to get up from their desks. They sat there and ate their crackers and maybe socialized a bit." At the lunch break, the children were almost unmanageable. "I asked the teacher why they didn't get a break to move around and go outside," she recalls. The teacher said the children got a few minutes of recess after lunch.

Troubled, Barros began collecting data on children, recess, and behavior. In 2005, Barros, now an assistant clinical professor of pediatrics at Albert Einstein College of Medicine, and a team of other doctors conducted a massive study looking at how much recess eleven thousand kids between the ages of eight and nine were getting every day. Her results, which were published in 2009 in the prestigious peer-reviewed journal *Pediatrics*, showed that 30 percent of schoolchildren in that age range had little or no daily recess. Kids from low-performing schools and poor neighborhoods tended to have less recess than kids who attended middle-class schools. What is the impact of denying kids a break? Dr. Barros and her team examined the record of those children who were denied recess and compared it to those who had daily recess to see if there was a link between better behavior and recess. She found that those who had more than fifteen minutes of recess a day showed better behavior in class than those who had little or none, even when researchers controlled for sex, ethnicity, pubic or private school, and class size.

Barros says her data is unequivocal—all elementary school children need twenty minute of recess each day.

"Think about it! Five- and six-year-old children in a room for four hours—looking at a book—without a break! That doesn't make sense. When parents look at schools for their children, they need to examine the recess schedule," says Barros. "An elementary school that doesn't have recess is not a good school. Parents should look elsewhere."

There are tantalizing clues that free play that includes vigorous movement may improve academic outcomes. Since the 1990s, scientists have been studying the human brain's ability to produce new brain cells—a process known as neurogenesis. The process is controlled by a protein called BMP (bone morphogenetic protein) found in the tissues of the body. The more BMP floating around in your bloodstream, the fewer new brain cells you produce. Exercise, it has been shown, clears away BMP like a broom and allows other brain proteins that spark growth to flood the brain and brain cell growth to flourish. For years, scientists have been able to show that animals who exercise more have larger brain mass and brains that function more efficiently. On a battery of rat-appropriate intelligence tests, rats who run on treadmills outperform rats who lie around in the cedar chips.

But children are not rats. Does exercise make children smarter? Some early studies suggest the answer may be yes. The fitter a child is, the better she seems to be able to perform on tests measuring short-term focus and also complex memory creation and retrieval. In one preliminary study out of the University of Illinois at Urbana-Champaign campus, researchers found that children who are fit have larger basal ganglia, which is the part of the brain that controls attention and that oh-so-critical executive functioning that allows humans to prioritize input, pay attention, and smoothly transition from one task to another.

A word of warning: it is easy to fall into the trap of thinking of the human brain like a simple machine. Measuring brain formation and connecting it to behavior or performance, though, is a tricky business. Measures of brain structure can show us changes that may or may not be significant. Measures of brain efficiency are conducted using technology that is more open to interpretation than most non-scientists realize. Studies that show that exercise can improve a child's performance on a particular test are interesting, but scholastic achievement is more complicated than that. With the limits of neurological research in mind, let's look at other kinds of studies that examine the connection between kids' opportunities for recess and physical education and their academic achievement.

One study that examined large populations of kids was conducted in 2001 by the California Department of Education. Reading and mathematics scores from the Stanford Achievement Test were matched against fitness scores for a group of 954,000 fifth, seventh, and ninth graders. Researchers found a positive relationship between physical activity and higher grades in school. But *fitness* is a broad word. Kids can be strong, but have a limited aerobic capacity. What works best?

Some researchers at the University of Illinois at Urbana-Champaign set out to answer this question: They found a medium-size school district in an urban community. Then they selected four out of the eleven schools in that district to participate in this study so that their sample most closely resembled the economic distribution of the country.

Two of the schools had a strong academic track record and two did not. The researchers used two fitness measurements: One measurement was used to identify muscle fitness, aerobic fitness, aerobic capacity, and body composition. The other measurement included a twenty-minute run at progressively higher speeds, a muscle fitness test that involved push-ups and curl-ups, and a sit-and-reach-for-your-toes type test of flexibility. Then they compared the fitness scores of the 259 participants with their scores on the math and reading parts of the Illinois Standards Achievement Test.

After researchers analyzed their data, they determined that in broad strokes, their results supported the study done by the California Department of Education: children who are physically fit do better on achievement tests. When the researchers combed through their data more carefully, they determined that being strong and flexible had almost no effect. However, kids who had a large aerobic capacity—able to run on a treadmill at faster and faster speeds, for instance, and, to a lesser extent, whose body mass index (BMI) was within a normal range, did better on reading and math achievement tests.

Add to this picture some preliminary but important data: there seems to be emerging evidence that making sure your child is at the peak of aerobic fitness by the time he gets to high school will maximize his life success. A bold claim, no? But if you dig down into research conducted by some epidemiologists in Sweden, it seems like aerobic capacity is linked to intelligence and a whole lot of other positive outcomes.

In 2010, the Swedish government ended 109 years of compulsory military service. But before that time, nearly every eighteen-year-old male Swede was required, if not to pick up arms, then at least to take a military screening test for strength and aerobic capacity. In 2007, Swedish researchers stepped into this treasure trove of data to see if there were long-term connections among fitness, cognitive functioning, and life success. In all, they looked at 1.2 million young men at eighteen years of age, about 97 percent of the male population of Swedes born between 1950 and 1976. Out of that group, 268,496 were siblings—with 3,147 of those being twins and 1,432 being identical twins.* The researchers compared the fitness data from those young men to national databases that tabulated information on school achievement, educational attainment, and occupational information.

Here's what they found: male subjects between the ages of fifteen and eighteen whose cardiovascular fitness was on the upswing—getting better all the time—exhibited greater intelligence scores than subjects with decreasing cardiovascular fitness. Of course, it could be that the chicken came before the egg—that smarter adolescent boys run around more. But the scientists hypothesized that the opposite is true—the better your child's cardiovascular health, the better his cognition will be. And here's why you really want to encourage your kid's middle school to bolster PE and give the adolescents some active recess time: longitudinal analysis of the same data showed that physical fitness at age eighteen predicted occupational status and educational achievement as the subjects aged. The fitter kids are at eighteen years of age, the better they do in life.

There is a tension between these two piles of research. And the competing pressures are what makes your child's school principal look so harried. Data about time on task suggests that the more instruction kids get, the more they learn. At the same time, there is mounting evidence on the connection between movement and peak cognition. At this moment in time, school administrators, for the

---

* Siblings are always juicy subjects for researchers in these big studies because sibs will be brought up in the same neighborhoods and usually attend the same schools. Twin studies—especially when they can compare fraternal and identical twins—are even more potentially revealing because researchers can compare outcomes in the two kinds of siblings and figure out, at least in a broad way, what role nature and what role nurture might be playing.

most part, emphasize instructional time. Teachers sometimes go overboard. These days, it can be difficult to persuade teachers—even elementary school teachers who are finely attuned to the needs of our youngest learners—to give kids the opportunities to move around. Principal Layne Hudes, who runs the Concord Road Elementary School in Ardsley, an affluent suburb of New York City, boasts that her staff is among the best. Still, in a community that prides itself on the large number of public school students who attend competitive colleges and universities, Hudes must continually urge her teachers to give students more opportunity to stretch, run around, and take in fresh air on the playground. "We have meetings twice a week where we discuss kids who are hard to handle in a classroom and mostly it is kids who very active," says Hudes. "Although our teachers know that these children—indeed all children—do better with frequent breaks, it is hard to get them to schedule regular breaks in the school day. They perceive that breaks—five minutes, ten minutes, twenty minutes of recess—will significantly reduce the time they can spend teaching our dense curriculum and it will ultimately lower the test scores." Hudes's message is a simple one: the more rigor you add to a curriculum, the more you need to add activity. "The two have to go hand in hand."

THE TAKE A WAYS

1. Kids need recess. They need break time. They need to move around. Not just little kids—even middle schoolers and high schoolers. The science is clear. Can we stop debating this now?

2. Longer school days and a longer school year can help schools teach students more. But the impact is not the same on all children.

3. Summer vacation, which can be enriching for middle-class kids, can be hurting the achievement of poor kids. Many parents need to rethink what kids do in the summer. Our schools need to provide more options.

4. More time spent in class is not going to help your child if that time is wasted on noninstructional matters like attendance, bake sales, pointless busy work, and dealing with behavioral problems.

5. In elementary school, twenty minutes or more of recess a day is the minimum. Doctor's orders.

6. Yoga in the classrooms is all well and good, but increased aerobic activity is associated with better learning outcomes.

7. By the time your child is in high school, she should be at her aerobic peak.

CHAPTER SEVEN

TEACHERS MATTER

LAW AND ORDER AND EDUCATION

It was a courtroom scene that would be familiar to any fan of *Law & Order*. True, there was no dead body, no murder weapon, and no last-minute confession. But the outcome of these court proceedings would rock the city just the same. The question at hand? Should New York City school officials be allowed to release data that pinpointed—by name—which teachers were effective at raising their students' test scores and which were not?

On the bench in the modest Manhattan courtroom, Judge Cynthia Kern, who sported an eye-catching head of curls, listened carefully as lawyers engaged in the legal version of a bare-knuckle brawl. Representing the teachers union was Charles Moerdler, a colorful New York character and a former city buildings commissioner who, incongruously, speaks with a slight British accent retained from a childhood spent in England. Moerdler argued that the rating system was developed as an internal education tool to help principals evaluate their staff, not as a scorecard for the public. If the city was going to release the results, the teachers' names should be redacted, he argued. The data was too limiting and too likely to be flawed to risk ruining the reputations of so many hardworking civil servants. "The issue is this: you can put anything into numbers," he told the court. "What went in was a subjective opinion. Out came a number. It didn't cease to be subjective because you turned it into a number. . . . Garbage in, garbage out." Besides, he pointed out, the data was collected under an agreement between the city and the union that it would stay secret. Releasing it would cause irreparable harm to the reputations of teachers.

On the other side were lawyers for news organizations and the city. The media knew that releasing the data would be a hot story. David Schulz, an attorney representing the newspapers, argued that it was in the public interest to release the data on employees paid out of public coffers. Issuing the effectiveness scores without teachers' names "means you don't know what's happening at the classroom level," Schulz said. "It means you can't evaluate how the Department of Education is doing its job. Those are all things the public has a legitimate right to know."

Lawyers for the city, where officials are eager to press for school reform, agreed. The city had made no secret of the fact that tough economic times meant that thousands of the eighty thousand teachers in the city were about to get laid off. This kind of data published in a five-part series in the *New York Times* and tabulated on an easy-to-access Web site would encourage parents to look more critically at exactly who was standing up in front of their kids' classrooms. The chancellor's office wanted to give parents the information they needed to fight to keep effective teachers in their kids' schools, which could disrupt the old last hired–first fired rule and, instead, find a way to fire bad teachers first. Official hoped the downturn in the economy coupled with the teacher-effectiveness data would create an opportunity to improve teacher quality by getting rid of poorly performing teachers.

But as in many highly charged debates around school reform, the nuance of the matter was buried. Most reporters who crowded into the courtroom knew that the data was not definitive—there are serious questions about the way teacher effectiveness data is compiled. And even when the numbers crunchers rule out the statistical "noise," which is what they call misleading data that doesn't follow a trend, teacher effectiveness in raising test scores often varies from year to year. Still, no one could deny it was powerful ammunition. A rating system—especially one based on test score numbers—would quickly become a quick and dirty way to create heroes and villains in the complex system of public education.

Weeks later, Judge Kern sided with the city and news organizations and ruled that the data should be released. Lawyers for the unions vowed to fight on to keep it secret. But whatever the outcome in the future, the city had won the battle in the short term: anyone who read a newspaper, clicked on a news Web site, or watched a local broadcast about the court hearing or the ruling knew that the Department of Education had evaluation data on each teacher who worked for the city. The news accounts of the trial hammered home the point over and over: some teachers were good and some were bad. The genie was slowly seeping out of the bottle

THE GOOD TEACHER

For the last couple of decades, our schools and many of our children have been kept from their true academic potential by a deforming myth: that all teachers are created equal. Although we freely recognize that there are good and bad doctors, lawyers, engineers, cleaning ladies, and chefs, in the bizarre universe of your child's school, teachers are all uniformly good. Each and every one. Here's what we are supposed to believe: teachers earn a teaching certificate, then enter their profession with sharp skills and an uncanny level of know-how to get the best out of all kinds of kids.

A group of remarkable education reformers came up with a name for this myth—they call it the widget effect, as in "Teachers can be treated as interchangeable widgets." And the implications of the teacher-as-widget idea, reformers argue, have been corrosive and prevented our schools from adapting to the changing educational needs of our country. When kids are not learning enough, the widget myth lets everyone off the hook. How? It works on a few levels.

First off, the widget myth works for the people who run our schools—superintendents, principals, and assistant principals. It allows them to be detached from what happens in the classroom. Because teachers are supposed to have the same level of skill, there is no need to provide them with regular evaluation that pinpoints their strengths and weaknesses. Principals can deal with the disciplinary problems that get sent to their office, organize the bus schedule, set up an after-school program, or figure out how to communicate with parents of students who speak only Urdu. Principals or assistant principals are under no obligation—professional or moral—to methodically help teachers improve their practice or to fire bad teachers (which, by the way, is next to impossible under most districts' union-negotiated work rules). Once or twice a year, principals organize teacher development days—teachers get a paid break from teaching, listen to a lecture or attend a workshop, come in to school late and leave early—but very little of that intervention is ever targeted by a teacher's managers to produce better outcomes in students.

It works for teachers, too, sort off. As I mention above, it allows teachers unions to press for work protections unknown in other industries. On a school-by-school level, it promotes a kind of superficial collegiality, too. In a school where the widget myth prevails, for example, a good teacher could not demand that a colleague do better, even when the evidence that he or she is hurting kids is clear. A second-grade widget won't turn to a first-grade widget and say, "What the heck did you do last year? Nearly half of the kids you sent me in September aren't reading at grade level!" because teachers are all widgets and failure to get kids to progress rests with all teachers, not just the ones who can't deliver good instruction. At a school that promotes the widget myth, the prevailing thinking in the teachers' lounge is, "I'm okay. You're okay. It's the kids who, for a variety of reasons, just aren't learning."

The widget myth also keeps parents from asking important questions about their children's education. If our teachers are widgets, then they are all supposed to have the same level of skills. That means any teacher can teach anything. And yet we watch with unease as this plays out in our children's schools. You drop your daughter off on the first day of fourth grade and, surprisingly, you find that last year's first-grade reading specialist is her lead teacher. Ask her what training she got for the new job and, more often than not, she'll just shrug. It's an awkward, hard-to-interpret moment. Here's what's happening: your daughter's fourth-grade teacher knows she's supposed to pretend that she's a widget.

In fact, the widget myth allows us all to look at teaching as just a job—like stenographer—and not what it really is, a wonderful combination of a gift and a craft. It encourages us to see one teacher as about the same as another, to smile tolerantly at those hyper parents who jockey to get their kids in front of one particular teacher or another. When we let these myths affect our relationships to schools, it is our kids who lose out.

TEACH YOUR CHILDREN WELL

Since the 1970s when we started keeping good records of national achievement rates, researchers have been trying to discover the Holy Grail of education—the answer to this riddle: What makes some students achieve and others fail?

As you have seen, well-run schools are key. A top-notch curriculum that embeds important learning in interesting, lively lessons is vital. But even under ideal circumstances, some kids do well and others stumble. What allows some kids to flourish in elementary and middle school, master a rigorous high school curriculum, and go on to college while other kids begin to fall apart in middle school, enter a downward spiral, and limp through high school, drop out, or worse? What can we do to maximize learning for all children?

For a long time, researchers and pundits placed most of the blame for underachievement on the most obvious factor: poverty. Poor kids in general do much worse at school than middle-class kids. The Hart and Risley research we looked at in chapter 2 showed that poor kids do enter school with some cultural and linguistic deficits. For the last forty years, academics have detailed the uncertain, insecure, and sometimes chaotic lives of poor families and the circumstances that make it difficult for poor children to succeed in school. After years of scrutinizing downtrodden families—specifically welfare moms—often single black women who lived in public housing—for their children's academic weaknesses, political activists and, later, researchers began to see the schools those poor kids attended as an instrument of their downward trajectory. Pundits began arguing that the schools serving low-income kids were also chaotic—with badly paid, minimally prepared, irregularly recruited, and inexperienced teachers. Those lackluster teachers were partly to blame for the large numbers of poor kids who were failing to learn.

But in the middle and late 1990s, some researchers—most notably Stanford University economist Eric Hanushek, who had been researching teacher quality for a long time, and statistician William L. Sanders—put this notion under a microscope. And here's what they found: good teachers matter more than just about anything else in education. You can raise teachers' salaries in poor schools, replace crumbling facilities with shiny new buildings, throw a flotilla of intellectually enriching supports around poor children, but if you don't have good teachers, poor kids won't do well in school.

So what is the effect of great teachers on all students? In a 1996 paper, Sanders and Sandra Horn from the University of Tennessee College of Education, Health, and Human Sciences took data that the state had collected between 1990 and 1996 for all three million second- through eighth-grade kids in the state and plotted their progress in mathematics, reading, language arts, science, and social studies. Using what is called a *value-added system*—a complicated formula that compares the test group of kids with a control group of kids with similar backgrounds, abilities, and achievements and predicts the growth for the test group in a particular subject—Sanders was able to pinpoint which teachers moved kids forward the most. And they found that the children who are assigned the best teachers have a tremendous advantage in school. It didn't matter if the children went into the excellent teacher's class already getting gold stars or barely passing. An excellent teacher helped her students do better than their counterparts in the so-so teacher's class—first the poor students, then the middling ones, and then the best ones.

The effects of getting good teachers year after year seem to be cumulative. In his study, an average math student who, by luck or by parental hectoring, managed to get the most effective teacher three years in a row was 50 percentile points above the average math student who only got the mediocre teacher.

And tragically, Sanders found the inverse is also true: even top students assigned to an ineffective teacher or even a so-so one did not keep pace with the students in the good teacher's class. Low-achieving kids assigned to ineffective teachers suffered the most. And those effects—both the positive and the negative—were long-lasting. Two years later, the researchers could still discern the effects of a good teacher on the students. The damage a bad teacher did to a child's trajectory was also evident two years down the line. "Groups of students of comparable abilities and initial achievement may have vastly different academic outcomes as a result of the sequence of teachers to which they are assigned," Sanders wrote. The idea that some teachers were better than others found its way into the massive federal education legislation that has shaped American schooling—No Child Left Behind. The law called for "highly qualified" teachers in every classroom. But how *highly qualified* was to be defined was an open question.

Since then, reams of research have pointed out that schools serving poor kids have more ineffective teachers. And more effective ones could close the achievement gap between rich and poor and black and white kids in this country. A 2002 study of teachers in Texas found that "having a high quality teacher throughout elementary school can substantially offset or even eliminate the disadvantage of low socio-economic background." A 2006 analysis of Los Angeles public school data concluded that "having a top-quartile teacher rather than a bottom-quartile teacher four years in a row may be enough to close the black-white test score gap."

Some economists compared what kids assigned to the least effective teachers learned with what kids assigned to the most effective teachers learned. They found that kids assigned to the most effective teachers advanced nearly a year farther ahead of their poorly taught schoolmates.

A highly effective teacher, it seems, should have a price above rubies. Labor economists, who take numbers and use them to create projections of financial outcomes, estimate that when you compare two reading classes of twenty kids each, a highly effective teacher adds between $300,000 and $760,000 to the class's potential earning power by instructing in a way that allows them to learn more.

Of course, statistics without context are a dangerous thing. In certain corners of the country, reformers (who usually don't spend too much time in classrooms) talk about good teachers as if, when freed from union constraints, they can single-handedly wipe out the lasting effects of poverty, joblessness, illiteracy, and substandard housing. More moderate reform factions support the idea of rewarding good teachers. But they also point out that if we acknowledge that there are good teachers like there are good doctors, lawyers, and chefs, then we have to accept that not all good doctors, lawyers, and chefs produce the results we may want every time. Sometimes a good doctor's patient dies. Sometimes an excellent lawyer's client goes to jail. Even gifted chefs can't consistently make gourmet meals without the proper tools and good-quality ingredients.

These days, some of the most influential names in education policy begin and end any conversation about reform with a discussion of teacher quality. "Highly effective teachers are crucial to student success," said Secretary of Education Arne Duncan in 2009 when he announced $49 million in grants aimed at improving the way teachers are prepared for the job. But there is much that is unknown. How do you find good teachers? Although their pension benefits are enviable, the starting salary for teachers is notoriously low. Is simply paying them more enough? How do you reward them so they'll keep teaching? And how do you get the so-so ones to teach better? In 2009, after spending nine years and $2 billion trying to increase high school graduation rates by breaking large schools into smaller ones, mega-philanthropists Bill and Melinda Gates announced that the educational wing of their foundation would change direction: instead they would spend $335 million—and a promise of more to come—to support school districts that were coming up with innovative ways to figure out what highly qualified teachers looked like and how to make more of them. "Let's focus on the thing that actually matters the most, which is the teacher," said Melinda Gates in a conference call to reporters.

School superintendents in New York, Nashville, Houston, Baltimore, and Denver, among many others, are trying to come up with a system to isolate the worst teachers and pinpoint the best and reward them with more money. In Los Angeles, when the *Los Angles Times* published the teacher effectiveness data collected by the school district there, reformers rejoiced, saying the articles were a big step toward identifying and rewarding the best teachers and getting rid of the bad ones. The teachers union called the data unreliable, incomplete, and unfair—and called for a boycott of the paper.

To be sure, independent research suggests that the so-called value-added data systems that many districts use to identify excellent teachers is less than perfect. One report by the highly regarded research group Mathematica looked at the results of the teacher-ranking system for the District of Columbia public schools and found that over three years, about one in four average teachers were misclassified as high performing. The data can also be highly volatile: a report by the Economic Policy Institute, which looked at the ranking system in five districts, found that two-thirds of the teachers who ranked in the top 20 percent one year fell out of that category the next. One-third of those deemed "highly effective" sank to the bottom 40 percent the following year.

There have been real human costs to what can seem, at times, like an arcane debate. Shortly after the series ran in the *Los Angeles Times*, one teacher, whose name appeared in one of the articles, took his own life. Union representatives suggested that he was a dedicated teacher who had become despondent after being unfairly tarred by incomplete and misleading data.

In that New York courtroom, that teacher's suicide was on everyone's mind. "The city of L.A. did this routine. And a teacher jumped off a bridge. Do we need that?" union attorney Moerdler asked the judge.

CHOOSING WISELY

So should parents make sure their child gets a great teacher every year? The data would indicate that it is very important. It is also hard to do. Most parents don't realize until they raise the question in their own school that they are stepping on the scholastic version of the third rail. Corporate communications specialist Ilene Shore learned just how difficult a conversation it could be when her son, now a middle schooler, was in first grade. She'd paid top dollar for her three-bedroom town house in Rockville, Maryland, an affluent community in Montgomery Country just outside of Washington, D.C., because the public school system there had such a strong reputation. "We assumed, naively in retrospect, that all the teachers would be uniformly good ones."

First grade went smoothly but at the end of first grade it was becoming clear that her son, Ben, was struggling to regulate his impulses. Although he mastered most subjects with ease, he fidgeted constantly. More often than not, he called out answers instead of raising his hand. His second-grade teacher was at a loss about how to handle him—and often resorted to scorn and shaming in order to control his behavior. Near the end of that school year, Shore went to talk to the principal, hoping to have a discussion about which third-grade teacher had background and experience to get the best out of Ben. The principal told her that "it was against the school's policy for parents to lobby for one teacher or another." It turned out that Shore's child was in a school that could have been called Lake Wobegon Elementary. All the teachers, the principal told Shore, were above average.

Cowed, Shore accepted the third-grade teacher her son was assigned.

The next year, though, was worse. Then, in fourth grade, Shore left her corporate job and began working as a substitute teacher at an elementary school that served poor kids not far from her home. "What I observed from being on the inside of a school is that just like employees everywhere, skills that teachers brought to work each day varied wildly. Just like in corporate America, there were some who were fantastic—who could get a job done and done well. And there were others who did just enough to get by." And here's what bothered Shore particularly when she thought back on how the principal had dismissed her concern: everyone who worked in the school where Shore worked knew exactly who the good teachers were and were not.

Back at her son's school, Shore started making discrete inquiries, asking other parents and teachers with whom she had a good relationship to figure out which fourth-grade classroom teacher might be the best match for her son. Then she returned to the principal's office to ask, once again, that her struggling son be placed with a teacher with whom he might click. Again, she was rebuffed. Shore has watched with a sinking heart as her son has become disengaged from school and fallen further and further behind.

Defending the widget myth ends up being part of a principal's job. National Association of Elementary School Principals president Barbara Chester explains how difficult it can be. Principals are charged with hiring the very best teachers and, between tenure and school work rules, dismissing a teacher after his or her probationary period is very difficult indeed. Yet the research on teacher hiring shows that it is damnably hard in the interview process to figure out who is going to turn out to be an excellent teacher. Principals, flying near blind in the hiring and limited in their ability to remove bad teachers from the classroom, are forced to defend those hires even when they recognize that the teacher is not producing results for kids. "Admittedly, there are teachers in the classroom who should not be there. No principal should have to cover for a bad teacher. But, of course, many do. No one says this job is easy," says Chester with a stiff laugh.

So if principals have a hard time figuring out who the good teachers are, what kind of chance do parents have? The research shows that many of the things people think should make a good teacher aren't as important as you'd think.

THE CHEAT SHEET

Where are the good teachers? Everywhere you look. And the bad ones? In classrooms right next to them. Research into teacher effectiveness shows us that schools in high-poverty areas tend to have less effective teachers. But at the same time, greater variability has been found within schools than between schools. The chances are that there will be some good teachers almost everywhere you look. But how to identify them? Here are some guidelines:

Certification: Every state requires that people who want to teach in public schools go through a process of certification or licensure. In most states, that means teachers must attend state-approved schools of education and complete thirty to thirty-five credits in education courses. At the end of that time, the wannabe teacher submits his or her transcript, the courses are added up, and the teacher is given permission to stand in front of a classroom. Once in a while, teachers come to the profession through other means—called alternate certification—which usually involves training in another profession and then taking some education courses in order to obtain a master's in education degree. The certification process is expensive and inconvenient, especially if you consider that a significant body of research finds no connection between student achievement and how teachers are certified. That's right. A teacher's license does not indicate whether he or she will turn out to be a good teacher or not.

Advanced Education Degrees: In most school systems, teachers who earn advanced degrees in education get paid slightly more. It is not uncommon for a teacher to put in a full day at school and then attend classes at night to get a master's or even a doctorate in education. Their stamina is impressive and their ambition is commendable. Sadly, an advanced degree in education, researchers say, doesn't necessarily make your child's teacher a good one. (A note on advanced degrees: If your child's high school teacher has an advanced degree in the subject he or she is teaching—mathematics or physics, for instance—that's a good sign. Advanced degrees in the subject a teacher is teaching have been associated with better outcomes for kids.)

Experience: She's new. She's young. She's energetic. But if it is her first year on the job, you probably do not want your child in that class. Yes, every teacher has to learn somehow. If you have an option for a decent teacher with a few more years of experience, you should go with the latter. First-year teachers in general—even ones who are going to turn out to be educational ninjas—do a poor job of moving student achievement forward.

In general, a good second-year teacher is better than a good first-year teacher, but not as good as a good teacher with substantial experience. By four years on the job, a teacher has usually reached the top of her game. If she is good she may stay good for years and be a credit to her profession. Or she may burn out and become a so-so teacher. If she is not a good teacher after four years, she may stay on the job but is unlikely to improve.

Highly Verbal Teachers Wanted: Remember in the preschool chapter when we talked about how important it is that the earliest teachers speak clearly and often? Highly verbal teachers are in fact a gift to students in every grade. Study after study finds that effective teachers score higher on tests of verbal ability.

And Highly Intelligent Ones, Too: It might seem obvious, but there is a strong connection between how well teachers do in school and whether they turn out to be effective teachers. Countries that do a great job at teaching their kids have figured this out already. In 2007, a study by the management consulting firm McKinsey & Company compared the backgrounds of teachers from the highest-performing school systems in the world. The results were bracing for Americans, to say the least. The report they issued on their findings, "How the World's Best-Performing School Systems Come Out on Top," noted that in South Korea, Singapore, and Finland, 100 percent of teacher candidates are drawn from the top third of their high school and college class. By contrast, in the United States, only 23 percent of new teachers got decent enough SAT scores back in high school to be considered in the top third of their class. Among new teachers in high-poverty schools, just 14 percent had SAT scores that put them in the top third. On top of that, study after study has found that teachers who attend more selective colleges produce higher student achievement.

Sometimes a teacher looks great but turns out to be a dud. You need to meet with the teacher to find out if there is a way you can better support your child's learning at home. (For pretty much any problem, you'll need to approach your child's teacher first.) Still not working? You need to meet with a principal to discuss your concerns. If you need to, seek out help from the district. Don't be put off. You know the research now. You know what is at stake, especially if your child is performing at less than grade level.

GOOD SCHOOLS GROW GOOD TEACHERS

When parents take a tour of the school, they are shown the bells and whistles: maybe the school has a well-equipped theater, a sunny lunchroom, or some state-of-the-art technology like smart boards. But there is a rarely discussed feature of a school, one that remains all but invisible to parents, that separates good schools from the not-so-good ones. What is it? The best schools have come up with a school-wide process to develop and retain excellent teachers. They provide serious and intensive mentoring programs and multilevel teacher evaluations that include evaluation of test scores, class observation, and parent and student surveys. It's one of those behind-the-scenes things that good schools do to ensure that their students have a better chance at success.

Many schools conduct grade-level or department-wide seminars in which master teachers openly discuss classroom dynamics with less experienced colleagues. Sometimes, this takes the form of an active mentorship program between teachers. In some schools, this includes a bulging file cabinet where experienced teachers archive their lesson plans so that newer colleagues don't have to reinvent the wheel every day for 180 days. In other schools, teachers form study groups to read deeply on various topics—say, controlling behavioral issues or instructing kids on the finer points of long division—in order to refine their own practice.

An elegant version of this is called Lesson Plan Study. Not long ago, I drove about an hour outside of Manhattan, to the leafy green campus of the Greenwich Japanese School, to see it in action.

The Greenwich Japanese School in Greenwich, Connecticut, has many unique attributes that make it seem like an unlikely model for an American school. For starters, it serves about 190 kids and almost all of them are affluent. Unlike the plain cinder-block construction of so many public schools, the Greenwich Japanese School is housed in a series of grand clapboard and stone buildings on the sprawling campus that were built to house an exclusive all-girls boarding school called Rosemary Hall. The classes are taught in Japanese. Most of the parents are Japanese nationals who have been transferred to oversee Japanese business interests in the United States.

One reason they enrolled their children at GJS is that while most of the children are bilingual, Japanese is their first and dominant language. But they also send their children to GJS because there is a strong perception that Japanese schools are more rigorous—the school year, for instance, is longer and starts in April. The curriculum, particularly in math, is pared down, sequential, and intense. Since the parents are planning to return to Japan, they don't want their children to risk being handicapped in Japan by having attended inferior schools in the United States.

One of the key ways that the Greenwich Japanese School keeps their level of instruction high is through Lesson Plan Study, a program of self-study and gradual improvement that provides teachers with a road map to excellence. It's an idea that is gaining traction in the United States. In 2009, about twenty teachers and principals from the area attended the Greenwich Japanese School Lesson Plan Study Open House. In 2010, about eighty public and private school teachers and principals from around the Northeast gathered to figure out how they might transplant this program, which is common in Japan, to their own schools.

The underlying notion of Lesson Plan Study is that accomplished teachers create high-achieving students. So far so good. But here's where Lesson Plan Study gets really interesting. The administration at the Greenwich Japanese School believes that all teachers need to work toward excellence in their craft, both individually and together. The group collectively identifies the order of the lessons. Then the group figures out which lessons, explanations, and techniques are most highly effective. They dissect that lesson, explanation, or technique, teach it to each other, and then record it in a thick, homemade-looking book for junior teachers to use as a guide when they enter the classroom. An added bonus: these lesson plans ensure that curriculum is taught in a logical sequence. That would be a nice change for American schools, which, even as states tighten their standards, tend to have a more scattershot approach. It is not uncommon for a schoolkid to revisit the study of, for example, the Iroquois four times in her kindergarten through eighth-grade history curriculum and spend a total of two weeks studying ancient Rome.

On a warm day in November, a group of about forty American teachers from around the Northeast were being shown how it's done. Teachers in the United States are often worried or intimidated when visitors walk through their doors—in fact, in most schools so little formal evaluation actually takes place that an official visit usually means trouble. Not so at the Greenwich Japanese School. Lesson Plan Study demands that all classrooms be open for regular observation from staff and other teachers. Today, the visitors were handed a map of the school and encouraged to visit different classrooms and, with the help of a translator, sample ongoing lessons. The teachers welcomed the chance to be seen at what was clearly the top of their game: their lessons were well-prepared, purposeful, and crisply delivered.

In one class, a fourth-grade teacher was helping children understand the role of adjectives in language using a simple line drawing of a whale. It consisted of a half-moon crescent (the whale's body) and a much smaller triangle (the whale's tail) resting on a horizontal line (the ocean). Through a series of questions, the teachers elicited from the children verbal descriptions that express this image most precisely. "The ocean is represented by a line," offered one young boy. The teacher turned the horizontal line vertical. "Going from side to side in the middle of the page," amended the child. "A horizontal line," added the teacher. The class nodded.

Later, her lessons will be subjected to dozens of analytic questions by other faculty members. Why did the teacher allow the children to see the line drawing of the whale before she explained the topic of the lesson? Why did she correct one child and let another's partially correct answer stand? Couldn't that be confusing?

In the teachers' lounge in most U.S. schools, this kind of second-guessing would set off a wave of defensiveness and self-doubt on the part of the teacher (and possibly a flurry of calls to the union delegate). That isn't the case in a school that uses Lesson Plan Study. "It encourages teachers to learn from one another, to share ideas," explains Katherine Traester, a math coach at Hamden public schools in Hamden, Connecticut, which has been adopting Lesson Plan Study into their district. Makoto Yoshida, who received his Ph.D. from the University of Chicago and is popularizing Lesson Plan Study in the United States, says that it is about "learning the method of a good explanation."

Lesson Plan Study undercuts the widget myth because it assumes that teachers can and will get better if they are given a chance. It is also a sign of a school that understands and values good teaching. Ask questions about how a school identifies, encourages, and enhances good instruction. If your child's school is not embarked on this in a methodical and serious way, some of the teachers your child gets will be good and others less so, but largely, it will be a crapshoot. And that's not good enough.

THE TAKE AWAYS

1. Find out how many first-year teachers are heading classrooms in the school in September. How many last year? If you can't get those numbers from the principal, this should raise your suspicion. If those numbers seem high, you are probably looking at a school in transition. Proceed with caution. Many experienced teachers? Don't get complacent quite yet. You can read that two ways: Either schools are holding on tight to their good ones (and this is particularly hard to do for schools in poor neighborhoods, since good teachers tend to migrate to schools in wealthier areas). Or the supervisors believe their staff are widgets and aren't

making an effort to evaluate teachers, identify the good ones, and ease the bad ones away from kids.

2. Be impressed with the marching band, the art room, and the new Apple computers. But also ask questions on your tour about teacher evaluation. For example, how do administrators evaluate the teachers? How often are classroom lessons observed?

3. See if that school is run by widgets. Ask the following: Can you describe an example where you determined a teacher was weak in a particular skill set? What did you do to address that?

4. Ask a teacher where she did her undergraduate work and what she studied. This is not snobbery. As a rule, teachers who graduate from more selective colleges—public and private—get better results out of kids.

CHAPTER EIGHT

THE PERFECT SCHOOL

WHAT WOULD A perfect school look like? The curriculum in every class would be tightly organized and properly sequenced. The instruction would revolve around best practices. In areas where there are none, teachers would translate up-to-the-minute innovations in cognitive science into the classroom. Well-trained and well-supervised teachers would deliver flawless instruction to their classes of twelve students. There would be plenty of time for recess, a robust history and science program, plenty of time for recess, and a decent art and music program to boot. Administrators would be well versed in the best thinking in education.

And as you've probably figured out by now, there's no such thing as a perfect school. Fortunately, our kids don't need one. Most of us would be satisfied to send our children to a good school. All around the country, parents from all walks of life are finding ways to make the good school a reality.

It's a transformation that doesn't happen overnight. When Linda Aponte and Jason Cohen first visited their local elementary school in Brooklyn, they weren't sure what they'd find. They knew that many of their neighbors took extreme measures to keep their kids from going there, opting for waivers to high-performing public schools or vying to gain admission to private ones. The Aponte-Cohens checked the test scores—they were not in line with what you'd expect in an economically mixed neighborhood like the one where they lived. "Not terrible," says Jason, a lawyer who has a short boxed beard and an open face, "but considerably below what you'd expect from our neighborhood." On the tour, Jason noticed the building was old but that it was clean and well maintained. There was no gym. The outdoor space was a square of concrete. The curriculum seemed to Cohen to be weirdly threadbare, focusing almost exclusively on math and reading. The arts were clearly an afterthought: on the tour, the principal introduced the music teacher, an elderly woman, as "someone who took the kids off the teacher's hands for forty-five minutes once in a while," recalls Jason. The art teacher was a parent trained by a nonprofit arts organization who did projects with the kids like gluing googly eyes on cardboard. As for science? There wasn't any. They took a deep breath and enrolled their daughter, Alycia. "We were prepared," say Jason and Linda together, "to put energy into the school to make it better and doing whatever we could to help our kids."

When Alycia was in first grade, Jason found a way he thought he might contribute. The district asked the school to form a School Leadership Team, a sort of advisory counsel made up of teachers, parents, administrators, and the principal. Cohen, who knew and liked the principal and had become a familiar figure around the school, ran for the job and won. Suddenly, he found himself immersed in a stream of information about the budget, curriculum, and management. The more he learned, the more uncomfortable and worried he grew. Although it would have been nearly impossible for a regular parent of a grade-school kid to see it, from his new vantage point on the School Leadership Team, he learned that aside from a huge emphasis on teaching kids reading and math, the school's curriculum was not consistent from class to class. Worse, there was no effort to create a progression in the curriculum from grade to grade.

The reading instruction most teachers were using had been unchanged for the last two decades. "About the reading program, well, I had an open mind," says Jason. Maybe the oldies were the goodies, he thought. "So I asked the principal why she had the teachers doing what they did." Her response, though, startled and dismayed him. He pauses, then describes it in measured, lawyerly terms. "It was clear that she was not even interested in entertaining the question. She just wasn't engaged."

Personally, he liked the principal. She had run the school for a long time. But was she doing her job? Jason began to watch her closely. The more he worked with her, the more he saw that she defined her job not as an educational leader but was focused on maintaining order in the school.

Then came the day when the School Leadership Team began discussing the school's teacher-review policy. No teachers the team spoke to could recall ever being reviewed—and the records showed that none had ever been given a negative review.

Jason and some of the other parents on the School Leadership Team tried to talk to the principal about some of their concerns. "When we brought it up she said, 'Yes yes yes,' waved her hand, and nothing happened," said Jason. By then, their second daughter was also attending the school. Linda had continued to rally support to expand the curriculum beyond reading and math. The principal appointed a teacher to instruct children in science, so Linda and a team of other parents cleaned out a large, sunny classroom that was being used as a de facto storage space, in order to create a dedicated science room. "What was in that room got put in a Dumpster and hauled away," she recalls. The teacher filled it with plants, terrariums, bits of bark, and interesting stones. She started a library of beautiful science books the children could select. Around that time, Linda and other parents formed a committee to launch school-wide ecology projects like recycling, planting trees, and keeping their streets clean.

For his part, Jason began digging into the budget. While teachers constantly complained that there wasn't enough money for enrichment activities, Jason found that the principal had resources available to her—funding streams, boxes of supplies and textbooks—that had gone unopened, unused, and unspent.

Jason and Linda had some dark nights. Like many of the parents on the School Leadership Team, they were demoralized. Their local school, which they thought they could improve, seemed mired in poor management and low expectations.

Jason, however, wasn't ready to give up on their neighborhood school. In frustration, he and some of the parents on the School Leadership Team drafted a letter to the district and Jason and some other parents hand-delivered it. Jason tells the story: "A group of us went to the district office and to our surprise, the district supervisor greeted us warmly. He said very openly that our school had been of great concern to him for some time." He said, Jason recounts, "that he'd wanted to change things at this school but he'd had difficulty doing anything because *no one had ever complained about it*. There were no letters in the file on that school that would support him taking any particular action." Jason said their group of activists was stunned. Would their single letter make a difference? It seemed too good to be true. "He said he'd work with us to see what could be done."

Over the next year, the district sent monitors to review the school's budget and management records, observe the school in action, and interview the principal, teachers, and parents. Sensing that the long-time principal was under fire, some parents rallied to her support. But by then, Linda and Jason had become convinced that the school could only improve with new leadership.

The Cohen-Apontes, though, drew back from the fray. Still, Jason kept attending the School Leadership Team meetings and quietly pushing for accountability and, when he could, change. "Did it happen fast? No," says Jason. And that was a mixed blessing. "We wanted improvement but not disruptive change."

About a year after the School Leadership Team delivered the letter to the district and six months after the district took effective control of the school, the principal opted to retire. An interim principal came in and some of the longtime teachers left. Attracted by the new leadership, a new wave of parents from the neighborhood started enrolling their children. Those parents made enough noise so that the school was given a face-lift and the outside yard was redone. These days, the interim principal is the principal. The school boasts a vibrant, coordinated curriculum with ample teacher training and connections between classrooms. The children are exposed to history, music, and art, and there is a full-time science teacher who runs a much-talked-about program. Each year, the older children go on field trips to an ecology center. Not long ago, they participated in a Trout in a Classroom project, where they learned about water conservation and released a trout into a cleaned-up stream. Parents from all walks of life—wealthy, middle-class, and poor—support the school. It is now one of the most desirable in the city.

The gains of the school, the Aponte-Cohens acknowledge, came mostly after their older daughter moved to middle school and nearly too late for their younger, who only enjoyed a couple of years of schooling under the new regime. But Linda and Jason don't regret their involvement.

"To me, the lesson other people might want to learn," says Jason, "is that there are rules and laws and that parents have significant rights to be engaged and have an impact." Sometimes, he says, it's not enough to complain. "It's good to get on the inside and try to make an impact from there." And have patience.

It turns out that an important hallmark of a good school is one where parents are active and engaged, not just in bake sales and candy drives, but in substantively supporting the school and encouraging it to be its best. All around the country, parents like the Aponte-Cohens are considering their children's educational options very carefully and making the best choice. And if there is no good choice, they are making or remaking schools for their kids. The aim of these activist parents is self-serving, at least initially: they want to improve options for their children. But they end up supporting or creating institutions that benefit many children. Forming a constructive coalition with your child's school can seem like an insurmountable challenge. For those of you who feel harried, distracted, and overstretched, here's a road map:

KNOW YOUR STUFF

Many of us feel like we are not sufficiently informed about matters of education. If you've made it this far in this book, you are on your way to becoming a more sophisticated member of your child's learning community. As you move further down the path, you'll probably find yourself seeking out more information and research.

Be choosey. There is a difference between magazines that run articles about new theories in education and scholarly journals that conduct peer review and contain empirical evidence about teaching and learning. Even in peer-reviewed journals, one study means almost nothing. Look for evidence that is replicated by other researchers. Look for consensus within the research community. At www.thegoodschool.org, we're on a mission to help parents get and stay better informed about education. Come and visit us.

And know this: you can never stop learning. True scientific knowledge is not dogma. It is public and open to challenge. And it is not set in stone. Scientific knowledge is subject to change when contrary evidence emerges.

DON'T BE PART OF THE NEW STUPID

Understand, too, that research and data only take us so far. As we saw in our discussion about testing in chapter 2, there is a longing in all of us to simplify this complicated business of education into a number, or a series of numbers, or a report card. That's a mistake. In a brilliant essay published in the journal *Educational Leadership*, conservative educational reformer Frederick M. Hess writes about the dangers of believing only the numbers. "A decade ago, it was disconcertingly easy to find education leaders who dismissed student achievement data and systematic research as having only limited utility when it came to improving schools or school systems." That attitude, writes Hess, was the "old stupid." "Today's enthusiastic embrace of data has waltzed us directly from petulant resistance to performance measures to a reflexive and unsophisticated reliance on a few simple metrics. . . . The result has been a nifty pirouette from one troubled mind-set to another: with nary a misstep, we have pivoted from the 'old stupid' to the 'new stupid.'"

Let's try and avoid the new stupid. While we want our children to have the best and most carefully tested programs and instruction, we need to use data and research as a way to frame some probing questions. We need to use it to identify best practices. But let's be sophisticated about how we use it.

BE RESPECTFUL

We must engage the schools that serve our children with respect. It is easy, even fashionable, to be harshly critical toward educators. Having spent years interviewing school administrators and teachers at all levels of education, I can tell you: they have hard jobs. Running a school is not child's play. It's not something you can "make up as you go along" and expect to get good results. To do it well requires the planning of General Patton, the communication skills of Soledad O'Brien, the energy of Lance Armstrong, and the patience of Mother Teresa. Few ordinary mortals get it all right all the time. There will inevitably be mistakes. But hopefully, those mistakes don't go on too long or become too large and can lead to an evolution in thinking.

We need to support the people who educate our children in all the ways that we can. Sometimes, though, aspects of education need to be improved. When you approach your child's school with an issue, try to walk a line between being forceful without being destructive. If your child is enrolled in a school, you'll need to follow the hierarchy of responsibility. As I've mentioned, the first person to talk to is your child's teacher. No satisfaction? Widen your circle: perhaps a learning specialist, perhaps a guidance counselor, perhaps an assistant principal, and finally the principal, a district leader, or a superintendent.

THERE'S STRENGTH IN NUMBERS

It is always useful to call upon the experience of other parents, in particular parents who have had older children in your child's school, for support.

Remember, too, there is strength in numbers. School administrators have a joke about activist parents: They say that one parent who is dissatisfied with an aspect of a school is a fruitcake. Two complaining parents is a fruitcake with a friend. Four complaining parents, though, are a force to be reckoned with. Within that dismissive bit of humor is a kernel of wisdom for parents. Schools serve a community. If large swaths of that community collectively push for change, your voices will be louder and more powerful than those of disgruntled but isolated individuals.

DON'T BE DRAWN INTO FALSE CHOICES

The debate over school reform is reaching a crescendo. And in many parts of the country, large industrial-scale schools are being broken up into learning academies, magnet programs are flourishing, districts are experimenting with online learning—all in the name of helping kids to learn more.

Students, once wedded to their neighborhood school or district, are pulling up stakes and their parents are applying them to what they hope will be better schools in nearby communities. In Massachusetts, a state that allows parents more flexibility than most, thousands of students are enrolling in schools outside their home district. In these budget conscious times, their adopted schools are only too happy to get them (the out-of-town students come with a $5,000-per-student subsidy taken from their home district).

Will any of these new options ensure that your child gets a great education? Unfortunately, it's not going to be that easy. In general, students from affluent neighborhoods tend to perform better than students from poverty-stricken ones. But plenty of schools in seemingly prosperous areas are struggling. To complicate matters, there is no "kind" of schooling that is going to be better than another. A poorly trained teacher in a magnet program or a half-baked curriculum delivered online is not going to help your child achieve. I believe we should welcome reforms in education—but not blindly. We need to keep our eye on the quality of education our children are receiving.

This holds true for charter schools as well. Originally conceived as an incubator for educational innovation, charter schools are now being held up, at least in some quarters, as the saviors of public education. They tend to be smaller than regular public schools. Their teachers, for the most part, don't belong to a union. "Supporting charter schools" has become a litmus test for politicians who want to be considered forward thinking on education. But charter schools are also highly variable.

When you visit a charter school like KIPP Infinity on West 133rd Street in Manhattan, it's hard to imagine a better school. KIPP Infinity sits in a dense, noisy, worn-out section of West Harlem. The regular public schools in that area are, at best, substandard.

By comparison, the six-year-old Infinity, which serves three hundred poor, black fifth through eighth graders, has been heralded as one of the very best middle schools in the city. It deserves accolades. An astonishing 100 percent of their eighth graders were rated proficient in math and 97 percent were rated proficient in the English language statewide tests. The classrooms crackle with energy. Teachers deliver well-planned lessons. Students, who get training on how to learn, are serious about performing at their peak. No matter what kind of neighborhood you live in, sending your child to a school like KIPP would be a dream come true. In the same Manhattan borough, some of the children of parents who pay $30,000 a year in tuition don't receive anywhere near the quality of education that KIPP students get for free. The operators of KIPP schools know what they are doing. They keep a sharp eye on student outcomes and are quick to reorganize a school that is not helping kids make gains. Not all charter schools are like this.

In roughly the same week that I visited KIPP, I heard from a second-year teacher who was working at a newly opened branch of a well-regarded charter school in Arizona. The teacher, Lindsay, described the kind of chaos that makes parents shudder.

Out of twenty staff members, Lindsay was one of ten who considered themselves novices. She'd been trained to teach seventh grade, but was switched to fourth grade days before school opened. She began the school year with no textbooks and only a sketchy idea of the curriculum she was supposed to teach. Day after day, she simply struggled to maintain order. "The class was filled with a lot of kids who weren't cutting it in their old schools, so they ended up here." Her classroom, which consisted of thirty-five kids, contained ten kids who had extreme behavior problems. Well-behaved students were being threatened by more aggressive kids in the hallways. Some parents quickly withdrew their children. Others seemed oblivious. "There was a lot of pressure to keep the doors to this school open," says Lindsay, "even when it was clear this was not in the best interest of the kids." Lindsay has been watching in disbelief as her failing school has thrown itself into marketing in order to attract more students for next year. "It's such a show," says Lindsay, "we recruited a bunch of kids who thought it was a great school. The parents really didn't know what they were choosing."

You may like the idea of charter schools. And indeed, there is much to like. And you may want to elect officials who create a political environment where charter schools can thrive. That seems like a good idea, too. But *charter school* is not synonymous with *good school*. There are good ones and bad ones. As parents, we need to be careful not to get drawn into false choices. If you want a good charter school for your child, you are going to have look carefully at how the school is run, what happens in the classroom, and how the school supports its best teachers.

As parents we share a powerful desire. It doesn't matter if you live in a mansion, a ghetto, or somewhere in between. It doesn't matter if you live in the city, in the suburbs, or in the country. No matter what our race, religion, ethnicity, or political persuasion, we all want our children to get the kind of education that will help them reach their full potential. It's universal.

Policy makers, foundation heads, union leaders, reformers, and teachers are beginning to realize that beyond the tumultuous, fast-moving, and often heated debate about education reform, parents have always wanted the same thing. The universal desire for our children to get a good education is being transformed from a potent yearning to a powerful political tool.

Will parents be able to effectively wield that tool? Only if we get smart and stay smart about education. Parents don't have a hope of sending their children to a good school unless they recognize what one looks like. I hope that this book gets you started on the process of finding one for your child.

NOTES

Introduction

1   *My parents used to say to me . . .*: "It's a Flat World, After all" by Thomas L. Friedman, *The New York Times Magazine*, April 3, 2005.

4   In the 1970s: A. Carneval, Nicole Smith, and Jeff Strohl, "Help Wanted: Projections of Jobs and Education Requirements Through 2018," Georgetown University, Center on Education and the Workforce, June 2010: http://cew.georgetown.edu/jobs2018/.

4   the National Bureau of Labor Statistics found: http://www.bls.gov/bls/unemployment.htm.

5   According to the National Center for Education Statistics: http://nces.ed.gov/fastfacts/.

5   Yet our reading scores: About a third of children in our public schools fail to become proficient readers: http://nces.ed.gov/pubsearch/pubsinfo.asp?pubid=2010458.

5   The World Economic Forum: J. Blanke, X. Sala-i-Martin, A. Franco, and T. Geiger, "Global Competitiveness Report: 2010–2011," http://www.weforum.org/issues/global-competitiveness.

5   The ACT administers subject tests: http://www.act.org/news/aapfacts.html.

Chapter One: The Preschool Scramble

23   In 2009, according: S. Barnett, D. Epstein, et al., "The State of Preschool 2009," National Institutes for Early Education Research, May 2010, http://nieer.org/yearbook/.

26   When he analyzed his data: W. Gilliam, "Prekindergarteners Left Behind: Expulsion Rates in State Prekindergarten Systems," Foundation of Child Development, FOC Policy Brief Series no. 3, May 2005, http://childstudycenter.yale.edu/zigler/publications/briefs.aspx.

28   In a 2005 analysis: S. Loeb, M. Bridges, et al., "How Much Is Too Much: The Influence of Preschool Centers on Children's Development Nationwide," National Bureau of Economic Research, December 2005, http://www.nber.org/papers/w11812.

29–30 In those days: For a fascinating book on early education, see Barbara Beatty, *Preschool Education in America: The Culture of Young Children from the Colonial Era to the Present* (New Haven and London: Yale University Press, 1995).

30   In Germany: Friedrich Froebel, *Kindergarten*, trans. J. Liebschner, ed. B. Watson (1844), www.friedrichfroebel.com/.

33   Around that time: For a compelling discussion of child development and neuroscience, see John T. Breur, *The Myth of the First Three Years: A New Understanding of Early Brain Development and Lifelong Learning* (New York: Free Press, 1999).

34   In 2011, the worldwide market: Barbara Wall, "Ambitious Parents Spend on Educational Toys for Toddlers," *International Herald Tribune*, November 24, 2006.

37   In 2001, researchers found: B. Hamre and R. C. Pianta, "Early Teacher-Child Relationships and the Trajectory of a Child's School Outcome Through Eighth Grade," *Child Development* 72 (2001): 625–38.

37   The American Psychological Association: American Psychological Association has this cool resource. Check it out: www.apa.org/education/k12/relationships.aspx.

38   We have two behavioral scientists: Betty Hart and Todd R. Risley, *Meaningful Differences in the Everyday Experience of Young American Children* (Baltimore: Paul H. Brookes, 1995).

42   Ello-Meno-Pee, 1, 2, 3: For a fascinating discussion on early reading skills, take a look at Marilyn Jager Adams, *Beginning to Read: Thinking*

and Learning About Print (Cambridge, Mass.: A Bradford Book, MIT Press, 1990). It's a classic. Also, if you have the time and the interest, I recommend Maryanne Wolf, *Proust and the Squid: The Story and Science of the Reading Brain* (New York: Harper, 2007).

43   Your child's ability: M. B. Denckla and R. G. Rudel, "Rapid 'Automatized' Naming (R.A.N.): Dyslexia Differentiated from Other Learning Disabilities," *Neuropsychologia* 14, no. 4 (1976): 471–79.

43   Researchers tell us: I. Lundberg, A. Olofsson, and S. Wall, "Reading and Spelling Skills in the First School Years Predicted from Phonemic Awareness Skills in Kindergarten," *Scandinavian Journal of Psychology* 21, no. 1 (September 1980): 159–73.

44   In one test conducted in the late 1980s: I. Lundberg, J. Frost, and O.-P. Peterson, "Effects of an Extensive Program for Stimulating Phonological Awareness in Preschool Children," *Reading Research Quarterly* 23, no. 3 (Summer 1988): 263–84.

47   In a study conducted: L. J. Schweinhart and D. P. Weikart, *Lasting Differences: The HighScope Preschool Curriculum Comparison Study Through Age 23*, Monographs of the HighScope Educational Research Foundation, 12 (Ypsilanti, Mich.: HighScope Press, 1997).

47   particularly boys: R. A. Marcon, "Socioemotional versus Academic Emphasis: Impact on Kindergartners' Development and Achievement," *Early Childhood Development and Care* 96 (1993): 81–91.

48   41 percent of the school day: C. Howes and A. G. Wishard, "Revisiting Shared Meaning: Looking Through the Lens of Culture and Linking Shared Pretend Play Through Proto-narrative Development to Emergent Literacy," in *Children's Play: The Roots of Reading,* ed. Edward F. Zigler, Dorothy G. Singer, and Sandra J. Bishop-Josef, pp. 143–58 (Washington, D.C.: Zero to Three Press, 2004).

49   In 2006, the American Academy of Pediatrics: www.aap.org/pressroom/playfinal.pdf.

54   According to a paper published in 2007: A. Diamond, W. S. Barnett, et al., "Pre-School Program Improves Cognitive Control," *Science* 318, no. 5855 (November 30, 2007): 1387–88; W. S. Barnett, et al., "Educational Effects of the *Tools of the Mind* Curriculum: A Randomized Trial," *Early Childhood Research Quarterly* 23, no. 3 (2008): 299–313. For a wonderful short book about the importance of play in preschool, seek out Kathy

Hirsh-Pasek, Robert Michnick Golinkoff, Laura E. Berk, and Dorothy G. Singer, *A Mandate for Playful Learning in Preschool: Presenting the Evidence* (New York: Oxford University Press, 2009).

Chapter Two: Testing

61 Gaming the SAT: www.businessweek.com/bwdaily/dnflash/feb2005/nf2005022_9320_db016.htm.

71 For a more detailed discussion of testing, check out Peter Sacks, *Standardized Minds: The High Price of America's Testing Culture and What We Can Do to Change It* (Cambridge, Mass.: Perseus Books, 1999); Daniel Koretz, *Measuring Up: What Educational Testing Really Tells Us* (Cambridge, Mass.: Harvard University Press, 2008); Stephen Jay Gould, *The Mismeasure of Man* New York: W. W. Norton & Company, 1981).

71 And testing's impact: Linda Perlstein, *Tested: One American School Struggles to Make the Grade* (New York: Henry Holt and Company, 2007).

Chapter Three: Class Size

75 According to the National Center: http://nces.ed.gov/fastfacts/display.asp?id=28.

76 Florida alone: http://www.hks.harvard.edu/news-events/news/press-releases/pr-pepg-research-may10.

78 Doug Ready: D. Ready, "Class-Size Reduction: Policy, Politics and Implications for Equity," Campaign for Educational Equity, Teachers College, Columbia University, 2008, http://www.equitycampaign.org/i/a/document/6863_Ready_Class_Size_Research_Review.pdf.

79 The other study: C. Milesi and A. Gamoran, "Effects of Class Size and Instruction on Kindergarten Achievement," *Educational Evaluation and Policy Analysis* 28, no. 4 (December 21, 2006): 287–313.

79 In 1985, researchers: B. Nye, L. V. Hedges, and S. Konstantopoulos, "The Long-Term Effects of Small Classes: A Five-Year Follow-Up of the Tennessee Class Size Experiment," *Educational Evaluation and Policy Analysis* 21, no. 2 (Summer 1999): 127–42.

80 Later analysis: A. Molnar, P. Smith, J. Zahorik, A. Palmer, A. Halbach, and K. Ehrle, "Evaluating the SAGE Program: A Pilot Program in Targeted Pupil-Teacher Reduction in Wisconsin," *Educational Evaluation and Policy Analysis* 21, no. 2 (Summer 1999): 165–77.

82   Six years later: http://www.rand.org/pubs/reprints/RP903.html.

83   Thomas Dee: T. Dee and M. West, "The Non-Cognitive Returns to Class Size" (working paper 13994, National Bureau of Economic Research, Cambridge, Mass., April 2008), http://www.nber.org/papers/w13994.

Chapter Four: Reading: What It Takes to Succeed

86   Some time: Jeanne S. Chall, *Stages of Reading Development* (New York: McGraw-Hill, 1988), pp. 15–27.

86   But in many schools: Here's a nice four-color graphic to explain it: http://nationsreportcard.gov/reading_2009/nat_g4.asp?tab_id=tab2&subtab _id=Tab_1#tabsContainer.

91   A federal report: http://nces.ed.gov/nationsreportcard/pdf/studies/ 2007482.pdf. Or later Victor Bandeira de Mello, Charles Blankenship, and Don McLaughlin, "Mapping State Proficiency Standards onto NAEP Scales 2005–2007," U.S. Department of Education, National Center for Education Statistics, October 2009, http://nces.ed.gov/nationsreportcard /pdf/studies/2010456.pdf.

91   For a really smart analysis of the gap between what's considered good by state and good by federal standards, go to http://educationnext.org/few -states-set-worldclass-standards/.

93   Reading scores are worse: http://nces.ed.gov/nationsreportcard/pubs /main2009/2010458.asp.

94   not reading at grade level in first grade: C. Juel, "Learning to Read and Write: A Longitudinal Study of Fifty-four Children from First Through Fourth Grade," *Journal of Educational Psychology* 80 (1988): 437–47.

94   Seventy-four percent: J. M. Fletcher and G. R. Lyon, "Reading: A Research-Based Approach," in *What's Gone Wrong in America's Classrooms*, ed. Williamson M. Evers, pp. 49–90 (Stanford, Calif.: Hoover Institution Press, 1998).

94   which in turn: C. E. Snow, S. Burnes, and P. Giffin, eds., *Preventing Reading Difficulties in Young Children* (Washington, D.C.: National Academy Press, 1998).

94   kids who struggle in reading: "Paying Double: Inadequate High Schools and Community College Remediation," Alliance for Excellent Education, Issue Brief, April 2006, www.all4ed.org/files/archive/publications/ remediation.pdf.

95 Reading problems: P. McCardle and V. Chhabra, *The Voice of Evidence in Reading Research* (Baltimore: Paul H. Brookes Publishing, 2004).

96 In 1839, statesman: Jonathan Messerli, *Horace Mann: A Biography* (New York: Alfred A. Knopf, 1972).

97 For a passionate if slightly dated discussion of the "pure phonics" approach to reading, check out Rudolf Flesch, *Why Johnny Can't Read—and What You Can Do About It* (New York: Harper & Brothers, 1955).

100 In 1967, Harvard Professor Jeanne: Jeanne Chall, *Learning to Read: The Great Debate* (New York: McGraw-Hill, 1967).

107 about one hundred hours: P. McCardle and V. Chhabra, eds., *The Voice of Evidence in Reading Research* (Baltimore: Paul H. Brookes Publishing, 2004), p. 36.

108 In 1987, the entire state: Diane Ravitch, *Left Back: A Century of Failed School Reforms* (New York: Simon & Schuster, 2000), pp. 443–47.

108 In a study conducted: K. Walsh, D. Glaser, and D. D. Wilcox, "What Education Schools Aren't Teaching About Reading and What Elementary Teachers Aren't Learning," National Council on Teacher Quality, May 2006, www.nctq.org/nctq/images/nctq_reading_study_app.pdf.

109 A few years ago: Robert A. Frahm, "Skills Test an Obstacle for Hundreds of Would-be Teachers," *The Connecticut Mirror*, February 10, 2010, www.ctmirror.org and http://www.westportnow.com/index.php?/v2/comments/new_skills_test_an_obstacle_for_hundreds_of_would_be_teachers/#more.

109 Anthony Pedriana: Anthony Pedriana, *Leaving Johnny Behind: Overcoming Barriers to Literacy and Reclaiming At-Risk Readers* (Roseville, Minn.: Learning Dynamics Press, 2009).

110 Out of all the states: www.jsonline.com/news/education/89007417.html.

111 If you are a community member and you're asked to help decide what kind of textbooks your school district should adopt, you can check out the government's marginally useful program and curriculum evaluation site: www.whatworksclearinghouse.com.

121 Kids who study words: G. A. Miller and P. M. Gildea, "How Children Learn Words," *Scientific American* 257, no. 3 (September 1987): 94–99.

122 Kids encounter an average: W. E. Nagy and P. A. Herman, "Breadth and Depth of Vocabulary Knowledge: Implications for Acquisition and Instruction," in *The Nature of Vocabulary Acquisition*, ed. M. G. McKeown

and M. E. Curtis, pp. 19–35 (Hillsdale, N.J.: Lawrence Erlbaum Associates, 1987).

122 For a high-minded and intriguing discussion of reading, reading research, and dyslexia, check out Maryanne Wolf, *Proust and the Squid: The Story and Science of the Reading Brain* (New York: Harper, 2007).

Chapter Five: When Mathematicians Get Angry

128 According to a 2008 report: "Foundations for Success: The Final Report of the National Mathematics Advisory Panel," U.S. Department of Education, March 2008.

128 According to the 2007 Nation's Report Card: "New 'Nation's Report Card' Shows NCLB Is Working for All Students," The Nation's Report Card, U.S. Department of Education, 2004, http://www2.ed.gov/nclb/accountability/achieve/2004-report-card.html.

129 Results from the 2007: "Foundations for Success," March 13, 2008.

129 In a study published: E. C. Melhuish, K. Sylva, P. Sammons, et al., "Preschool Influences on Mathematics Achievement," *Science* 321, no. 5893 (August 2008): 1161–62, http://www.sciencemag.org/content/321/5893/1161.short.

129 Researchers at the American Diploma Project: "Closing the Expectations Gap 2011," Sixth Annual Report, American Diploma Project Network/Achieve, February 2011, http://www.achieve.org/files/AchieveClosingtheExpectationsGap2011.pdf.

130 According to the National Science Foundation: www.nsf.gov/statistics/seind10/c3/c3h.htm.

130 Technology start-ups: Vivek Wadhwa et al., "America's New Immigrant Entrepreneurs: Part I" (Duke Science, Technology & Innovation Paper no. 23, January 4, 2007), accessed October 20, 2010, at http://ssrn.com/abstract=990152.

131 According to the 2007 Trends: http://timss.bc.edu/timss2007/index.html.

131 Stanford economist: E. A. Hanushek, P. E. Peterson, and L. Woessmann, "Teaching Math to the Talented," *Education Next* 11, no. 1 (Winter 2011): 11–18.

133 They could grasp: R. Gelman and R. Baillargeon, "A Review of Some Piagetian Concepts," in *Handbook of Child Development*, vol. 3, ed. J. H. Flavell and E. Markman, pp. 167–230 (New York: Wiley, 1983).

133 For a nice history of mathematics instruction, check out Diane Ravitch, *Left Back: A Century of Failed School Reforms* (New York: Simon & Schuster, 2000); Suzanne Wilson, *California Dreaming: Reforming Mathematics Education*, (New Haven, Conn.: Yale University Press, 2003); and Tom Loveless, ed., *The Great Curriculum Debate: How Should We Teach Reading and Math?* (Washington, D.C.: Brookings Institution Press, 2001).

134 In 1972, 3.6 million: From Wilson, *California Dreaming.* (Some of those students must have begun the study of math later in their high school career.)

136 Frustratingly, long-term trend data: "NAEP 2008 Trends in Academic Progress: Reading 1971–2008/Mathematics 1973–2008," The Nation's Report Card, U.S. Department of Education, 2008, http://nces.ed.gov/nationsreportcard/pdf/main2008/2009479.pdf.

140 In 2008: Justin Halberda, Michèle M. M. Mazzocco, and Lisa Feigenson, "Individual Differences in Non-verbal Number Acuity Correlate with Maths Achievement," *Nature* 455 (October 2, 2008): 665–68.

141 Subsequent studies: Justin Halberda and Lisa Feigenson, "Developmental Change in the Acuity of the 'Number Sense': The Approximate Number System in 3-, 4-, 5-, and 6-Year-Olds and Adults," *Developmental Psychology* 44, no. 5 (2008): 1457–65. Halberda, Mazzocco, and Feigenson, "Individual Differences in Non-verbal Number Acuity Correlate with Maths Achievement."

146 In his 1997 book: Stanislas Dehaene, *The Number Sense: How the Mind Creates Mathematics* (New York: Oxford University Press, 1997).

148 In a presentation given to the American: Genevieve Hartman and Wakasa Nagakura, "Reflecting on Reflections: How Better Understanding Preservice Teachers' Beliefs and Concerns Can Help Us Help Them" (paper presented at the symposium "Video Analysis as a Method for Developing Preservice Teachers' Beliefs About Teaching and Their Understanding of Children, Pedagogy, and Assessment," 2010 AERA Annual Meeting, Denver, Colo., May 4, 2010).

150 Turns out, about ten years ago: Harold W. Stevenson and James W. Stigler, *The Learning Gap: Why Our Schools Are Failing and What We Can Learn from Japanese and Chinese Education.* (New York: Simon & Schuster, 1992).

150 For more fascinating discussions of mathematics cognition and instruc-

tion, check out Liping Ma, *Knowing and Teaching Elementary Mathematics: Teachers' Understanding of Fundamental Mathematics in China and the United States* (Mahwah, N.J.: Lawrence Erlbaum Associates, 1999); and Brian Butterworth, *What Counts: How Every Brain Is Hardwired for Math* (New York: Free Press, 1999).

Chapter Six: The Right Balance

158 By the turn of the century: Joel Weiss and R. S. Brown, "Telling Tales over Time: Constructing and Deconstructing the School Calendar," *Teachers College Record* 105, no. 9 (2003): 1720–57.

159 By 1900, the nations' schools: D. Tyack and L. Cuban, *Tinkering Toward Utopia: A Century of Public School Reform* (Cambridge, Mass.: Harvard University Press, 1995), pp. 12–28.

159 Around that time: E. Silva, "On the Clock: Rethinking the Way Schools Use Time," Education Sector, Washington, D.C., January 11, 2007, http://www.educationsector.org/publications/clock-rethinking-way-schools-use-time.

160 summer vacation: H. Cooper et al., "The Effects of Summer Vacation on Achievement Test Scores: A Narrative and Meta-analytic Review," *Review of Educational Research* 66, no. 3 (Fall 1996): 227–68.

161 In a study released in 2010: V. Lavy, "Do Differences in School's Instruction Time Explain International Achievement Gaps in Math, Science, and Reading? Evidence from Developed and Developing Countries" (working paper no. 16227, National Bureau of Economic Research, July 2010).

163 In the late 1980s: Charles Fisher et al., "Teaching Behaviors, Academic Learning Time and Student Achievement: Final Report of Phase III-B, Beginning Teacher Evaluation Study, Technical Report V-1," Commission for Teacher Preparation and Licensing, Sacramento, Calif., June 1978.

163 Sometimes it's even worse: B. Smith, "It's About Time: Opportunities to Learn in Chicago's Elementary Schools," Consortium on Chicago School Research, December 1998, http://ccsr.uchicago.edu/publications/p0f03.pdf.

164 In 2006, a survey: J. McMurrer, "NCLB Year 5: Choices, Changes and Challenges: Curriculum and Instruction in the NCLB Era," Center on Education Policy (July 24, 2007), http://www.cep-dc.org/displayDocument.cfm?DocumentID=312.

165 Since then, though: "Access to Arts Education: Inclusion of Additional Questions in Education's Planned Research Would Help Explain Why Instruction Time Has Decreased for Some Students," United States Government Accountability Office, Report to Congressional Requesters, February 2009.

170 Dr. Romina Barros: Romina M. Barros, Ellen J. Silver, and Ruth E. K. Stein, "School Recess and Group Classroom Behavior," *Pediatrics* 123, no. 2 (February 2009): 431–36, doi:10.1542/peds.2007-2825, http:// pediatrics.aappublications.org/cgi/content/abstract/123/2/431.

173 Researchers found a positive relationship: California Department of Education, "2001 Legislature," Sacramento, Calif., James B. Grissom, "Physical Fitness and Academic Achievement," *Journal of Exercise Physiology* 8 no. 1 (February 2005), www.asep.org/files/Grissom.pdf.

174 Then they compared: Darla M. Castelli, Charles Hillman, Sarah Buck, and Heather Erwin, "Physical Fitness and Academic Achievement in Third- and Fifth-Grade Students," *Journal of Sport and Exercise Psychology* 29 (2007): 239–52.

175 The fitter kids: Maria Aberg, Nancy Pedersen, et al., "Cardiovascular Fitness Is Associated with Cognition in Young Adulthood," *Proceedings of the National Academy of Science* (November 30, 2009), doi:10.1073/ pnas.0905307106PNAS, http://www.pnas.org/content/106/49/20906 .full.

Chapter Seven: Teachers Matter

181 A group of remarkable: D. Weisberg et al., "The Widget Effect: Our National Failure to Acknowledge and Act on Differences in Teacher Effectiveness," The New Teacher Project, 2009, http://widgeteffect.org/ downloads/TheWidgetEffect.pdf.

184 In a 1996 paper: "Groups of students of comparable abilities and initial achievement may have vastly different academic outcomes as a result of the sequence of teachers to which they are assigned," Sanders wrote in Williams L. Sanders and June C. Rivers, "Cumulative and Residual Effects of Teachers on Future Student Academic Achievement," University of Tennessee Value-Added Research and Assessment Center, Knoxville, Tenn., November 1996; W. L. Sanders, A. M. Saxton, and S. P. Horn, "The Tennessee Value-Added Assessment System (TVAAS): A Quantitative, Outcome-Based Approach to Educational Assessment," in

Grading Teachers, Grading Schools, ed. J. Millman, pp. 137–68 (Thousand Oaks, Calif.: Corwin Press, 1997). William L. Sanders and Sandra P. Horn, "Research Findings from the Tennessee Value-Added Assessment System (TVAAS) Database: Implications for Educational Evaluation and Research," *Journal of Personnel Evaluation in Education* 12, no. 3 (1998): 247–56, doi:10.1023/A:1008067210518.

185 A 2006 analysis: For a good synthesis of the research, go to Kati Haycock and Eric A. Hanushek, "An Effective Teacher in Every Classroom," *Education Next* 10, no. 3 (Summer 2010): 46–52, http://educationnext.org/an-effective-teacher-in-every-classroom/.

186 They found that kids assigned: There is a great deal of incremental research on this, but for a nice synthesis with a rather breathless title, check out B. Hassel and E. A. Hassel, "Opportunity at the Top: How America's Best Teachers Could Close the Gap, Raise the Bar, and Keep Our Nation Great," Public Impact, 2010. The authors are consultants who work with charter schools.

186 Labor economists: D. Staiger and J. Rockoff, "Searching for Effective Teachers with Imperfect Information," *Journal of Economic Perspectives* 24, no. 3 (Summer 2010): 97–118.

187 In 2009, after spending: "Bill Gates Gets Schooled," *Bloomberg Businessweek*, June 26, 2006, http://www.businessweek.com/magazine/content/06_26/b3990001.htm.

187 One report: Peter Z. Schochet and Hanley S. Chiang, "Error Rates in Measuring Teacher and School Performance Based on Student Test Score Gains," National Center for Education Evaluation and Regional Assistance, Institute of Education Sciences, U.S. Department of Education, document no. PR10-29, 64 pages, Washington, D.C., July 2010, http://ies.ed.gov/ncee/pubs/20104004/pdf/20104004.pdf.

187 The data can also be highly volatile: S. Corcoran, "Can Teachers Be Evaluated by Their Students' Test Scores? Should They Be? The Use of Value-Added Measures of Teacher Effectiveness in Policy and Practice," Annenberg Institute for School Reform, Brown University, 2010, http://www.scribd.com/doc/37648467/The-Use-of-Value-Added-Measures-of-Teacher-Effectiveness-in-Policy-and-Practice.

190 Principals, flying near blind: Staiger and Rockoff, "Searching for Effective Teachers with Imperfect Information"; J. Rockoff, B. Jacob, T. Kane, and D. Staiger, "Can You Recognize an Effective Teacher When You

Recruit One?" *Education Finance and Policy* 6, no. 1 (Winter 2011): 43–74.

191 *Advanced Education Degrees*: M. Chingos and P. Peterson, "It's Easier to Pick a Good Teacher Than to Train One: Familiar and New Results on the Correlates of Teacher Effectiveness" (paper prepared for a symposium sponsored by the *Economics of Education Review*, June 28, 2010).

192 She's new: Steven G. Rivkin, Eric A. Hanushek, and John F. Kain, "Teachers, Schools, and Academic Achievement," *Econometrica* 73, no. 2 (March 2005): 417–58; Richard J. Murnane and Jennifer L. Steele, "What Is the Problem? The Challenge of Providing Effective Teachers for All Children," *The Future of Children* 17, no. 1 (Spring 2007): 15–43; R. Gordon, T. Kane, and D. Staiger, "Identifying Effective Teachers Using Performance on the Job," The Hamilton Project, The Brookings Institution, April 2006.

192 *And Highly Intelligent Ones*: M. Barber and M. Mourshed, "How the World's Best-Performing School Systems Come Out on Top," McKinsey & Company, September 2007, http://www.mckinsey.com/App_Media/ Reports/SSO/Worlds_School_Systems_Final.pdf.

Chapter Eight: The Perfect School

205 In a brilliant essay published in the journal: F. Hess, "The New Stupid," *Educational Leadership* (December 1, 2008), http://www.frederickhess .org/5136/the-new-stupid.

ACKNOWLEDGMENTS

I'd like to thank the Spencer Foundation and specifically Spencer president Michael McPherson and Paul Goren, now director of the Consortium on Chicago School Research, and the dean of Columbia University's Graduate School of Journalism Nicholas Lemann, for generously providing me with the support to "go back to school" and spend an entire academic year listening, reading, and thinking. I'd also like to thank Columbia's Dean Arlene Morgan, Professor LynNell Hancock, who oversees the program I attended, and Professor Marguerite Holloway, who acted as my adviser. They did their best to direct me that year—and showed me how to make the most of it. Their unflagging encouragement was invaluable. Elizabeth Green and Sarah Garland, two talented writers and thinkers, and Spencer Fellows from 2009 to 2010, were intelligent sounding boards and highly entertaining dinner companions.

My friends at Henry Holt have been the force that moved this project from a proposal to a finished book. Holt president Steve Rubin understood the power of *The Good School* right away. Holt

ACKNOWLEDGMENTS

executive editor Gillian Blake has been a sensitive reader and skilled editor and helped me in one thousand different ways. It has been wonderful working with you.

Along the way, I was the beneficiary of a great deal of encouragement from journalists Julie Scelfo, Barbara Kantrowitz, and Mary Suh, who let me explore a few ideas for this book in the pages of the *New York Times*. Katharine T. Barnes gets a special mention here, too, and she knows why. Every writer should have a friend with a beach house: my good friend Elizabeth Forero let me use hers so I could finish this manuscript. Thanks.

Praise and gratitude to my agent, Richard Pine from Inkwell Management, for his encouragement, enthusiasm, and guidance. I couldn't ask for better.

My heartiest and heartfelt thanks to all the parents, teachers, administrators, and researchers who so willingly gave me their time and their insight.

INDEX

ABOUT THE AUTHOR

PEG TYRE is the author of *The New York Times* bestseller *The Trouble with Boys*. She was awarded the prestigious Spencer Fellowship for Education Reporting at the Columbia Graduate School of Journalism where she began work on this book. Her writing about education has appeared in *Newsweek*, *The New York Times*, *Family Circle*, and iVillage.com. She lives in Brooklyn, New York.